# CULTURE SHOCK!
## Malaysia

**Heidi Munan**

**Graphic Arts Center Publishing Company**
Portland, Oregon

**In the same series**

| | | |
|---|---|---|
| *Australia* | *Indonesia* | *Singapore* |
| *Borneo* | *Israel* | *South Africa* |
| *Britain* | *Italy* | *Spain* |
| *Burma* | *Japan* | *Sri Lanka* |
| *Canada* | *Korea* | *Taiwan* |
| *China* | *Nepal* | *Thailand* |
| *France* | *Norway* | *USA* |
| *Hong Kong* | *Pakistan* | |
| *India* | *Philippines* | |

Illustrations by Nina Paley
Cover photographs by Jean Paley
Photographs by Jean and Hiram Paley,
Tourist Development Corporation of Malaysia,
Jabatan Penerangan Malaysia

© 1991 Times Editions Pte Ltd
Reprinted 1992, 1994

This book is published by special
arrangement with Times Editions Pte Ltd
International Standard Book Number 1-55868-070-5
Library of Congress Catalog Number 91-72722
Graphic Arts Center Publishing Company
P.O. Box 10306 • Portland, Oregon 97210 • (503) 226-2402

Printed in Singapore

# CONTENTS

# FOREWORD

Malaysia is a cultural potpourri for the casual visitor. Malays, Chinese and Indian dominate in Peninsular Malaysia while in Sabah and Sarawak — the Borneo states that make up the rest of the country — Kadazans and Dayaks add to the variety.

Tour groups are given glimpses of the colour and richness of traditional dances, music and food and they go away with photographs that capture the essence of their brief encounter with quaint alien cultures. The impression one gets is the greenery, the friendly people, the food, the nice hotels, the good roads and the relatively high standard of living. All very fleeting and very superficial.

But for the fairly large expatriate community that lives in the country, it means getting to really know the people and their culture. There is always a period of adjustments. The need to know and understand local customs in all its variety often gets driven home by trial and error. It is a learning process that takes time and depends on how well or how interested the expatriates are in wanting to blend into the local scene and not stand out, awkward and self-conscious.

Heidi Munan, the author, is well-placed to pick out the essentials, herself an expatriate, but who by marriage to a Sarawakian has made Malaysia her home. Her own personal experiences and the fact that hers was a case of learning by trial and error bring that insightful touch to this book spiced with humour that comes from pitfalls she herself may have encountered for want of being better informed.

There is the common story — not in this book — of the expatriate who was taken to a South Indian restaurant for lunch where he ate the banana leaf on which the food was placed, thinking it was the salad. That was his only grouse about the food – the salad was tough!

There is plenty in *Culture Shock Malaysia* to arouse interest. For the casual visitor coming into brief contact with the country and its peoples or the expatriate settling down for a couple of years or more, the book should provide a useful starting point, at least, of understanding the place, and making a stay there pleasant and satisfying.

Shiv Das
The New Straits Times Press
Malaysia

# ACKNOWLEDGEMENTS

In the 29 years I have lived in Malaysia, I have had many an earnest talk about the State of the Nation and what to do about it with folks from all walks of life. In the 12 months I devoted to doing research for this book, I asked more pointed questions, sought out new contacts to tell me what it's like to come here now, as a "new boy" or "new girl", and settle down for a few years. What do you need to know? What do you wish you'd known before you left home? What would you tell another newcomer, more recent than yourself? My daughter's college friends chipped in with under-20s views of our great land; it is through them that I discovered that to Indonesians, for instance, Malaysia is foreign territory indeed!

The fruit of all these labours, my own and my many informants', are distilled into *Culture Shock Malaysia.*

I would like to thank the Paleys for their generous assistance with the illustrations in *Culture Shock Malaysia.* Hiram and Jean are responsible for many of the photos, while their gifted daughter Nina drew the cartoons that add spice to my decorous pages.

It is impossible to thank all those who have helped me in one way or another with the compilation of this book. The names of many friends, old and new, who have spent hours patiently answering my questions, would fill pages. If I started naming a few aunts and cousins but omitted others there would be uproar! I prefer to say Thank You, and be assured your knowledge and advice will help our new friends settle happily in Malaysia.

Heidi Munan

# Chapter One

# A LAND UNITED BY THE SEA

## GEOGRAPHY

West Malaysia is the Golden Chersonese of antiquity, the Malay Peninsula. The Straits of Malacca separate it from Sumatra to the west; the South China Sea laps the East Coast. The Peninsula lies immediately north of the equator but below the hurricane belt. In the days of sailing ships, the harbours of the Borneo Coast and the Straits of Malacca were often used by traders to weather the monsoon storms which raged in the South China Sea.

Sarawak and Sabah, which make up East Malaysia, lie on that brooding island mass, Borneo. They are divided from the other half of Malaysia by the broad expanse of the South China Sea.

## The Climate

Malaysia has two seasons a year — wet and very wet. Rain falls daily during the monsoon season from September to December, but even during the supposedly "dry" time there are a couple of showers per week.

Kuala Lumpur recorded 185 rainy days in 1986, Kota Kinabalu in Sabah 167; Kuching in Sarawak holds the unenviable record of 248!

Air humidity is high all the year round, from 60% to 73% at two o'clock in the afternoon. Temperatures in Malaysia range from 25° C to 35° C, with mostly cool nights. "Cool" means that in hilly areas it is advisable to use a light blanket for night covering; in the low-lying parts a cotton sheet is enough.

In the lowlands, where the bigger towns are situated, Malaysia is hot, hot, hot. The traveller, the prospective sojourner, has to bear this in mind when making preparations for coming here. 24° C is considered to be rather on the cool side!

## The Land

The eleven states of West Malaysia extend from Johor in the south to the Thai border in the north, including a few offshore islands. Sabah and Sarawak in East Malaysia are perched on the northeast and northwest of the great island of Borneo, which they share with Indonesian Kalimantan and the Sultanate of Brunei.

The Peninsula's backbone of mountains, Banjaran Titiwangsa, runs north–south. Short rivers drain either into the Malacca Straits or the South China Sea.

The mountain range rises to over 2,000 metres in places and was a serious obstacle to east-west traffic in the past. A road from Kuala Lumpur to Kuantan was completed in 1911, another to Kota Bharu only after 1980.

All Malaysian states have access to the sea, from tiny Perlis Indra Kayangan (795 square kilometres) tucked away between Kedah

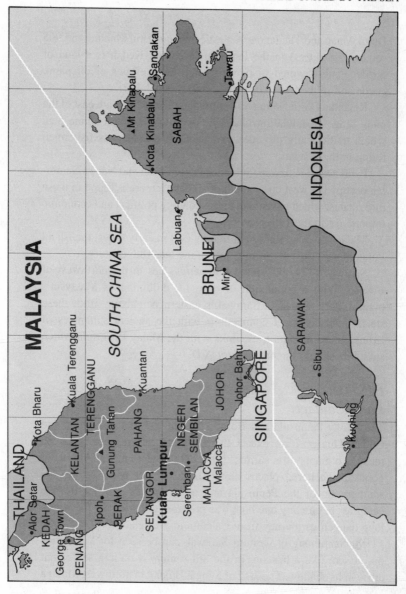

Darul Aman and Thailand to majestic Pahang Darul Makmur (35,965 square kilometres) in the Peninsula's centre. Kedah is a land of fertile plains devoted to rice growing; huge estates of oil palm, cocoa and rubber now cover the lowlands of Johor.

Kelantan Darul Naim and Terengganu Darul Iman are east of the main ranges. Undulating plains lie open to the South China Sea, which traditionally provides sustenance to the fearless fishermen living in these states.

Perak Darul Ridzwan, Selangor Darul Ehsan and Negeri Sembilan occupy the west coast south of Kedah. Tin ore is found in these three states, which gave them corresponding political and economic importance in the 19th century.

Malacca was an important trading port in early times; the island Pulau Penang rose to prominence in the late 18th century.

Sarawak (124,000 square kilometres) lies in the northwest of Borneo. With a population of only 1.9 million, it is Malaysia's biggest state. Sabah is Sarawak's eastern neighbour. Both these states have historical connections with the ancient sultanates of Brunei and Sulu, and trade links with the Malay Peninsula which stretch back into the 4th century A.D.

## HISTORY
### Early Contacts

The Malay Peninsula and Borneo lie half-way between India and China. This position makes them the natural entrepots between these two giants. It is surmised that early traders met and bartered goods in sheltered places along the Straits of Malacca, on the southern tip of the Peninsula and on the north coast of Borneo centuries before any one boat was prepared to undertake the whole long dangerous journey from Calcutta to Shanghai.

Mt Santubong in western Sarawak can be seen for kilometres out at sea, like a beacon; in the 8th century a trading settlement arose in its shadow. The area of Sungai Bujang in northwest Malaya was populated with traders; a lively manufacturing industry flourished here. Footpaths across the Peninsula were used to portage goods to the East Coast.

The foreign traders and settlers anticipated others who came centuries later: they brought their religion with them, their way of life, but they didn't settle in the country in significant numbers. Hinduism and Buddhism have left cultural traces, artefacts as well as customs which became absorbed into local folkways. Many Malay wedding customs may be traced back to a dim Hindu past.

Chinese traders joined these settlements, to exchange Indian for Chinese goods and to buy up the Peninsula's produce. It is from early Chinese historians that we know what goods were in demand, at what sort of prices, and how the 12th-century natives of the Malay Peninsula dressed and behaved.

While trading activity occupied the varying peoples of the coast, the jungle-fit aborigines roamed the Peninsula's mountainous interior in search of a livelihood. The earliest Malaysians were Negrito, ancestors of today's Semang and Jakun; invading groups of proto-Malays drove them further and further into the inaccessible hills and little is known of these people's history, preserved in chants and legends. The 19th-century scribes who compiled official histories of the various Malay states were mesmerized by the written word; we are only now learning to overcome the didactic view that "Malaysia's history begins with written records".

## *The Malacca Sultanate*

History according to the written records doesn't really start until the 14th century:

A princeling called Parameswara, exiled from his native Sumatra, founded a pirate base on Tumasek (Singapore) by the political expedient of killing its established chief. Being a less than popular ruler, he was later expelled and fled to the fishing village of Malacca where he made himself master.

Geography and the trade patterns of the day assisted Parameswara's undoubted abilities: Malacca grew into a trading centre important enough to attract the jealousy of the Siamese, and the protection of the distant overlord of most of Southeast Asia of the day, China.

Ambassadors bearing tribute were dispatched to the Ming court. Chinese seafarers visited the settlement, which continued to thrive and prosper. Numerous Indian traders settled in Malacca too. It was they who brought Islam to this area in the early 15th century. The history of Malacca under its Indianized Malay court is a tale of intrigue and heroism, poison and daggers, and unquestioning loyalty to the ruler. It tells of strong wily ministers like the famous Tun Perak who served five Sultans, one of whom was probably poisoned.

The last chief minister, Tun Mutahir, made the fatal mistake of trying to trick the Portuguese when they sailed into the Straits of Malacca in 1509. He took the advice of the leading Indian traders in town and launched a sneak attack on the foreign vessels in port. Most of the intruders escaped, only to return with reinforcements, ready and able to take revenge on the treacherous "Moors" as they called all Muslims.

## Portuguese, Dutch and English Influence

The Portuguese were the first western nation to show its flag in the Straits. They took Malacca in 1511 and built a Fort, a Church and a Customs House. But they did not live happily ever after. The exiled Sultan had established himself on Riau, an island south of Singapore, and tried to regain his dominion. Other powerful Malay States in the region, notably Acheh in northern Sumatra, resented the foreigners' rough and ready ways, and their attempts at creating a trade monopoly.

Sea rovers gained political control of Johor-Riau. Legitimate trade declined as bigger, better equipped vessels chose to sail west

*Legacy of the Dutch — Christ Church, an exquisite piece of architecture built in 1753.*

of Sumatra on their way to Batavia, rather than risk running the pirate gauntlet of Malacca Straits.

In the early 17th century the Dutch had established themselves in West Java. With active help from Johor, they took Malacca in 1641, and after this the town's importance declined rapidly. The island of Penang, acquired by the British East India Company in 1785, was the only important foreign trading base in the Straits.

15

Penang gave the British a foothold on the vital India-China route, which increased in importance as China Tea became a fashionable drink in Europe. Prizes were given to the captain and crew of the first ship to bring the year's fresh harvest to England; the period's tall "tea clippers" were marvels of speed and elegance under sail.

After the foundation of Singapore in 1819, the British intervention in the turbulent affairs of the Peninsula was practically inevitable. Too much money was at stake! Chinese immigrant tin miners and Malay rulers of various degrees of respectability kept up a steady turmoil in a potentially rich region. The British considered it their painful duty to intervene in Perak in 1843, in Trengganu in 1862. By 1874, all major tin-mining regions had been provided with Residents, British officials whose duty it was to advise the traditional ruler on all matters not pertaining to tradition or Islamic law, such as trade and foreign affairs. Refusal to take the advice was considered a serious matter, as the Sultan of Perak found out in 1875.

## The Beginning of the Modern State of Malaya

In 1905, Perak, Pahang, Selangor and Negri Sembilan were persuaded to unite as the Federated Malay States. This facilitated administration and commerce.

By the turn of the century, the Indian and Chinese communities were making their presence felt. Malay nationalism stirred in the 1920s; anti-British Chinese political parties were founded at the same time. Each local community was suspicious of the other, but all relied on the British to keep order.

Administratively, Malaya, as the Peninsula was then known, was a hodgepodge: Federated Malay States, Unfederated Malay States (under protection), Straits Settlements of Penang, Malacca and Singapore.

When the Japanese army overran Malaya in 1942, just under half the population were Malays. The Chinese made up a third, the Indians about 14 per cent.

The end of the war in 1945 did not bring a return of the good old days. Guerillas who had harassed the occupying forces refused to lay down arms, striving to replace the colonial government with a communist one.

An Emergency was declared in 1948. It dragged on for 12 weary years, holding the country in a state of siege, restricting population movement, free assembly and many other things usually taken for granted.

Malaya got its first Constitution in 1955, preparing for Independence in 1957. Three main political parties emerged: the UMNO (Malay), the MCA (Chinese) and the MIC (Indian). The first elected Prime Minister was a member of Kedah aristocracy, Tunku Abdul Rahman.

In 1963 Malaysia, a Federation of Malaya, Singapore, Sarawak and Sabah, was formed.

Singapore left Malaysia in 1965, and is now a Republic.

## *Exploring the Past*

This is a very brief overview of the rich and fascinating tapestry that makes up the history of the Malay Peninsula. A few specialized books are recommended in the bibliography.

But there is a way of studying history without books. Leisurely walks in the old parts of town reveal road names that are yesterday's Who's Who: Jalan Yap Ah Loy (*jalan* means road), Jalan Loke Yew and Jalan Rajah Abdullah take us back into the turbulent 19th century. Jalan Brickfields indicates the site where bricks were baked to convert the leaf-mat hovels of early Kuala Lumpur into an elegant new settlement, in the early years of the 20th century.

In any Malaysian town, the area around the major river is worth careful investigation. Rivers were the main traffic routes until the early 20th century. Often, the courthouse and the police station are near the river, or old warehouses with stucco-decorated window ledges and door frames; sometimes new cement structures serve as goods storage but a pair of old stone gateposts indicate where the older godown stood.

The Old Town is not usually suitable for driving; motorists avoid it unless they have specific business there. But take a bus down town. Bring a camera or a sketchbook. Wander in and out of the narrow lanes, look, learn, make use of a historically informed imagination! Stop at a little coffee shop, where a cool drink will be served at a marble-topped table while a ceiling fan whirrs creakily overhead.

Malaysia is a country where this sort of exploration tour may be undertaken by two or three foreigners, or even one on his own (though it's more fun with friends!), in perfect safety, in any part of town. The only danger that may lurk in crooked little side-streets is a bucket of water tossed out of a doorway, or a trishaw backing from a concealed entrance.

*Petaling Street, Old KL Town, provides an interesting glimpse of Chinatown where street vendors and old shop houses offer all manner of goods and services from fortune-telling to exotic Chinese medicine and herbs.*

— *Chapter Two* —

# FIRST IMPRESSIONS

## *A WALK IN TOWN*

Your first forays into the streets will be crowded with a bewildering tumble of impressions — this place is foreign all right! To start with, you are a stranger in town, whether you came here as a tourist or to settle for a few years.

### *Weather*

For one thing, it is hot. If you live in air-conditioned premises and normally use an air-conditioned car, it seems even hotter. But the heat is real. It's here to stay. You will have to learn to adapt to it.

Malaysian heat isn't of the killing, heat-stroke kind. It's seldom above 35° C, fairly humid; in big towns like Kuala Lumpur, the heat is overlaid by a haze of exhaust and industrial smoke. This is unpleasant but not life-threatening; solar topees went out with Somerset Maugham though sunglasses can help to keep the glare out.

Quite a few local people carry umbrellas to shield themselves from the sun. Hats, strangely, are seldom worn except by labourers or farmers. Visitors from overseas who are used to seeing hats as part of the school uniform often comment on the crowds of schoolgirls patiently sweltering in the heat at bus stops and pedestrian crossings. If ever there was a climate for straw hats, Malaysia has it — except that a panama hat wouldn't shelter its wearer from the very frequent showers!

Don't feel shy about using either a hat or an umbrella if you want to. The locals you see on the road are walking from A to B on the shortest possible route. You are strolling around town, possibly for hours — sunblock lotion and/or a sunshade may preserve you from a nasty sunburn.

This warning doesn't apply to the fair Caucasian skin only, but to anybody who is not used to the sun in generous quantities. Korean and Japanese visitors to the tropics do well to start off with protection; their children are very susceptible to burns, too! Start off with care, and get used to the sun slowly. There's plenty of it in Malaysia!

## Getting Around

Kuala Lumpur (or KL as it is fondly called) takes foreign ladies in shorts and halter tops calmly; in a country town this type of outfit may provoke comment. The conservative population will consider such shameless attire as yet another proof of the wicked western decadence they've been admiring on TV.

For walking in town, wear comfortable clothes, preferably of cotton or linen. Synthetics can make you feel very hot and sticky in a short time; natural fibres absorb perspiration instead. It is a good idea to wear sleeves, and not only for reasons of modesty. Clothing actually protects the wearer from the sun — who would prefer a bikini-sized sunburn to a shirt-and-jeans one?

Besides the heat, there's another danger in town: the traffic. Kuala Lumpur may not be a huge town by world standards, but there's quite enough traffic to get run over by. Use the pedestrian crossings and overhead bridges; they're there for your own good! And don't be surprised to have a bus pull up, practically on your toes, far from the nearest bus stop. That's the Minibus, a practical institution if you know how to use it and a deadly menace if you don't.

KL has a dense Minibus network, each number serving a specific route at non-specific times. What distinguishes them from "real" buses is their size, and their stopping places. A Mini is shorter than a standard bus, not air-conditioned, and it does not necessarily stop at bus stops.

*The Minibus is a practical and inexpensive way of getting around in the city. For those who want comfort and speed, use the taxi. Many local people go by trishaws when travelling short distances.*

Minibuses stop anywhere by the roadside. If there is a safety fence between the road and the sidewalk, the Minibus is likely to stop just outside that fence, preferably on a corner.

The practical meaning of all this is: when walking in town, stay on the sidewalk. Do not stroll on the road margin; ordinary traffic cuts it pretty near, and Minibuses pull right in to the curb anywhere their drivers sniff a potential passenger.

As a means of getting from A to B, the Minibuses are quite practical. The fare is 60 cents from anywhere to anywhere. The conductor will tell a passenger unfamiliar with the route where to get out if he is asked. There is such a thing as a KL bus timetable, and no home should be without one — not even if you own a car or generally use taxis. The timetable will only give the vaguest information as to when the bus will come, but it contains information about whence it cometh and whither it goeth after it has vanished around Chow Kit corner.

One word of warning: do not use buses during the rush hours! Rush hours affect the otherwise friendly Malaysian who tends to get impatient, especially in a jam-packed bus. Everybody seems to be wearing rubber slippers or tennis shoes in KL, except at 5.15 p.m. on a Minibus. That's when they're all shod in hob-nailed boots! The danger of being trampled on one's toes is very real.

In a small Malaysian town, a foreigner gets stared at if he's out for a quiet little walk. As this applies to small towns the world over, I don't feel obliged to apologize. In Malaysia's big towns, a person would have to look very remarkable indeed to get more than a passing glance.

Of course it will be fairly obvious that he is a foreigner, and a "stranger in town". This is not necessarily a bad thing. People will try to answer his questions and give directions. Carry a map! Many passers-by, people waiting at a bus stop for instance, will be happy to help you put it the right way up and tell you where you are.

The language problem may come into this. If there are senior

*A tourist police. Notice the name tag. Malaysian government officers wear them for easy identification.*

schoolchildren around, approach them. They do, theoretically, know English. A group will be less shy than one boy on his own; one girl on her own may turn up her nose in the air, or even take to her heels, if she's asked questions by a male stranger. Not many are as shy as all that, but it can happen.

Policemen in town areas should speak English. In the "tourist preserve" of Kuala Lumpur, a special "tourist police" is deployed; all members of this force speak good English. In an emergency, the combination of a map and some acting talent, plus slow careful enunciation of the place you are looking for, should work.

If all else fails, take a taxi. Malaysian cabs are saloon cars with yellow roofs. They are hailed by a Hitler salute from the kerb if there is no taxi stand nearby. Be sure the driver understands you before he puts his vehicle into motion — even in KL there are a few taxi drivers who don't understand English.

*Grazing animals, if untethered, are potential road hazards.*

## Stray Animals

People from countries where dog licensing laws are enforced will find the sight of stray dogs strange, not to say unpleasant. There is such a thing as an SPCA in Malaysia, but strays continue to flourish, if that is the right word to describe the sometimes miserably skinny, mangy creatures.

Of course your heart will be wrenched by the sight of poor little puppies and kittens crawling about in the gutters near open-air foodstalls. So will your children's hearts. Have a good excuse ready unless you want them to collect animals to bring home! Such charity is not recommended; most of these strays carry many different kinds of diseases and are vermin-infested. Try to ignore them, and leave them alone.

In rural areas, the nocturnal driver may find that the local cow and buffalo population has chosen the road for its sleeping accommodation. There may be a yellow "Beware of Cattle" sign by the roadside. If animals are seen in pasture near the road, keep an eye open for strays, their eyes shining in the glare of your headlights as they all turn to face the interesting diversion. They are probably lying down chewing their cud, so don't expect them to get out of the way quickly.

In theory, it is the farmers' responsibility to keep their cattle under proper restraint and prevent them from endangering public thoroughfares. In practice, hitting a cow can be a nasty accident, followed by an equally nasty farmer whose livestock you've just reduced by one. Of the two parties involved in the collision, the one who knows the Road Code is morally wrong even if he's legally right.

Another way of encountering animals on the road is in flattened form. Yukky, yes. Worth stopping for, no. Divert young children's attention from such melancholy sights if possible.

### The Crows of Klang Valley

An animal often noticed by newcomers is Kuala Lumpur's crows, seen everywhere in the urban spread of Klang Valley. They are comparative newcomers themselves, only observed in large numbers since the early 1980s. Nature observers often claim these large, strong birds are driving out some smaller native species. That may be so; they are also excellent scavengers. Housewives who put trays of food outside the house for sun-drying may find that the crows are more than just scavengers. They are accomplished thieves!

### Mind Your Handbag!

Not all thieves in a Malaysian town wear black feathers. In crowded places, pickpockets may be plying their trade. In recent years

25

there has been an unfortunate tendency for young children, trained by their elders, to be involved. They run through a crowd and "accidentally" bump into somebody; a chance passer-by kindly helps the victim to get up or steady himself — but the helper is a thief.

Avoid walking into the thick of a crowd, keep a tight hold on your handbag or camera, don't carry a wallet or a pack of banknotes visibly in a pocket. The best advice, here as anywhere else, is not to carry irreplaceable items like passports or air tickets when going for a walk in town. Things need not be stolen; it is perfectly possible to lose them, too.

## Beggars

The presence of beggars in the streets is another strange sight to people from the temperate lands. It doesn't mean the country is on the verge of starvation. Many beggars are handicapped in some way; the "village idiot" is allowed the freedom of the streets here unless he is dangerous, and he may do a little begging too. Blind beggars are seen seated outside the mosques, quietly chanting while waiting to receive the alms it is the faithful's duty to dispense. Elsewhere in town, blind musicians are merrily busking on sidewalks or in shopping malls.

Malaysians are, on the whole, a caring lot. A hardluck story in the newspaper inevitably brings in some donations for the victim. Families who can't afford to send a baby or child overseas for life-saving medical treatment may be able to raise a substantial part of such fees by a public appeal. The beggars you see in the street are begging, not starving; many coffee shop owners will treat beggars to a free meal for charity's sake. It costs three dollars on earth but will be worth treasures in heaven.

A number of children are seen begging, too, some clinging to their mothers' skirts, others fearlessly working the crowds and demanding as much as asking for alms. The activities of these youngsters distress not only sensitive foreigners. The Malaysian welfare authorities occasionally round up child beggars, especially those who are "working" for an "owner" who deploys them in the most promising spots around town. Some may be returned to their parents, or placed in orphanages if no parents can be found. Unfortunately, for every 10 thus provided for, another 10 spring up from somewhere...

## Jaga Kereta Boys

The *jaga kereta* (car watcher) boys do not normally harass pedestrians, but this is a good place to introduce them. "Boys" of any age from mid-teens to early sixties hang around parking areas, offering to guard cars while they are left there. If the driver declines such a perfectly useless service — unlike horses, cars may generally be trusted to stand still if left unattended — it will be politely pointed out to him that his car might get scratched or otherwise damaged during his absence. Much better employ a *jaga kereta!* Needless to say, these "watchmen" disappear fast if a policeman shows up in the distance.

## Girl Watching

Gangs of youths, of about the mental and educational level of *jaga kereta* boys, may amuse themselves by ogling, calling to and whistling at foreign women. They are mostly found hanging around shopping malls. If it's any comfort, they lavish their compliments on any women; local girls refer to them by the scathing term "lice".

Foreign females are a more obvious target because they look different, and they often walk on their own or respond to greetings from strangers. The attentions from these lads may be annoying but they are usually harmless. Take a leaf out of the young Malaysian women's book and walk past such pests, nose in the air, ignoring them completely. A friendly "hello" will only spur them on to further efforts in the "Hello darling!" and "Kiss me darling!" line.

## Eating Places

There are more than perils and dangers to strolling in the Malaysian town. There are pleasures for the eye and the ear (especially if you like five different tapes played at once within 12 metres of each other); the nose will spot those ubiquitous little eating stalls that waft tempting flavours over almost any outdoor situation in a Malaysian town. Provided there be a few square metres of space, there will be food stalls.

At first glance, they sell a bewildering variety of — what? Some things you'll easily recognize, others you're not too sure. The contents of that large pot look exactly like barley soup, for instance, but it's served over chipped ice and garnished with what seem to be diced fruit and jelly.

Yes it is barley soup, of a sweet variety, eaten because this grain is said to have cooling properites.

The first question one asks usually is: how do I order? For the tourist who is planning to live off stall food for a few days, the second question will be: how do I get a square meal?

You order by imitating others. Wander around the stalls, note where the food is chopped and sold by the plateful, where it is seethed or mixed and sold in a bowl, where it is tossed and fried and sold in a fragrant mound. Watch what other eaters order.

Go up to the food stall, and tell the seller you'd like some of what those people are having. Indicate them very discreetly, by pointing with your thumb or a crooked forefinger; pointing with a straight finger is considered rude. Then take a seat at one of the rickety little tables. A boy will come up to take your order for a drink, which is sold by a different stall. It is a good idea to drink frequently while strolling around town; until you are used to the fine variety of germs Malaysia has to offer, stick to bottled drinks.

Many foodstalls sell snacks only. After a few months here, you

*Malaysian colourful food stalls offer a splendid variety of delicious fare representing the multiracial makeup of its people.*

will wonder why Malaysians aren't hugely overweight, they seem to be snacking all day! There is a "*kachang putih* man", a seller of steamed peanuts or chick-peas, at every street corner. But if you are looking for a square meal, the chicken rice or "mixed rice" stall is your best bet, or the Indian *roti* seller who prepares piping hot pancakes which are served with curry. Here, too, you order straight from the seller. "I would like rice, and this, and this, and this" of the variety displayed in a glass case. Here, too, point with a thumb, a crooked finger or the whole hand, not a pointed finger. It doesn't do to be rude to your daily rice!

Some newcomers would dearly like to try stall food, but are worried in case it is fiery hot curry. Look around the other diners and see what they order for their children — that is probably the safest choice.

## Sidewalk Activities

Food stalls are not the only sidewalk activity. There are sidewalk cobblers who'll fix a lose heelplate while you wait; sidewalk fortune-tellers who'll promise you a golden future if you let them. Small shops spill over into the sidewalks, another lot of stalls, perched on the edge of the sidewalk so they nearly fall into the roaring cataract of the road, offer anything under the sun. Peddlers make their way through any crowd, offering you the cheapest ever Gucci bag, or a Rolex watch.

"Very, very cheap! The cheapest, sir! Genuine Rolex."

"Aw come on, this isn't a Rolex. It's an imitation!"

"Ah, but this is a genuine Rolex imitation, sir!" This is the sort of answer that may be worth 15 dollars to you, plus a fairly useless watch!

## Suburban Strolls

In suburban and *kampung* areas, evening strolling, with or without intention of looking for the local foodstalls and possibly a snack, is a general institution. Older houses have a little bench in front, or along the bridge that connects the lot to the road, for people to sit and enjoy the evening air. Old people sit there, younger ones stroll by with a few polite words of greeting; small children run everywhere. The idyll is only marred by mosquitoes, and occasionally an inconsiderate driver.

If a heavy afternoon shower cleared the air a couple of hours earlier, the evening is crisp and pleasant, the tangy smell of freshly quenched earth still lingering. Spicy cooking smells drift from the various houses, the sizzle of *sambal* and spices, the indefinable scent of the Orient.

# Chapter Three

# SETTLING IN — YOUR NEW ENVIRONMENT

It is likely that you will live in one of the bigger towns, probably Kuala Lumpur or Penang. There is plenty of housing available ... at a price. All of rural Malaysia is making a beeline for the urban conglomerations, and while the expatriate won't be in direct competition with this flood, he is affected by it indirectly. Housing at the lower end of the scale is getting more and more expensive, thus driving up rentals across the board. Unsightly and unhygienic "squatter settlements" disfigure the fringes of otherwise pleasant neighbourhoods and interfere with water supply and drainage. A shrewd owner or agent will not scruple to quickly bung a newly arrived expatriate into a house that no local tenant would want to rent, for good solid reasons!

Some expatriates have housing provided for them by their employer. It may be The Company House or Flat, eliminating all the problems of house-hunting or house-choosing. It may be a choice of houses or flats; if several are offered, the one vacated most recently is likely to be the most desirable. Many foreign employees are given a housing allowance, and told to stay in a hotel until they are suited. The following notes are mostly for them.

## HOUSE-HUNTING

To start with, get a map of the town in which you are going to live. With the help of an employee of your company, or a compatriot, mark down your place of work. Then eliminate places where you wouldn't want to live: the main industrial concentrations, too near the airport or the railway line, on low-lying swampy ground liable to flash floods, on very steep slopes. This will narrow the choice considerably, especially if you take the route to and from work, maybe the children's route to and from school, into consideration. The ideal house for you would stand at point X. Now comes the quest for the ideal house, with the help of an estate agent, radiating out from point X but never deviating too far. Don't let yourself be bullied into anything you don't really like, location or house!

Consider how big a house you will need. Have you a large family? Will you do a lot of entertaining at home? Do you like a garden, a swimming pool, a tennis court with the attendant problems of a gardener/caretaker? Do you prefer the modern style of house, or a gracius colonial mansion? Or is a luxury flat more in your line?

Make a list of all the things you desire in a home, and then contact an estate agent. Ask the senior staff in your employer's office to recommend an agent if you are not yet in contact with a community association. It is possible that the agent is a friend or relative of that staff member's; this is not necessarily a disadvantage. It certainly is "the Malaysian way of life", and the staff member will feel responsible for the honesty and ethics of the cousin in question. After all, you could complain to him daily for the rest of your stay in Malaysia if the house is not up to expectations!

Inspecting a prospective house is about the same chore in any country on earth. Check the plumbing and drainage; if the house lies in an elevated position (very pleasant for breezes), check the water pressure. Are there sufficient storage cisterns, water heaters? In a low-lying area water pressure will not be a problem; garden drainage may be. Most Malaysian houses have outside drainage even for the kitchen and bathrooms, so peer into the drains and see if they are full of stagnant water, debris, roots, blockages. It is also worth your while to find out whether the area is liable to flash floods during heavy rains.

Try out every tap, every switch, every gadget throughout the house. A fully-furnished house must have adequate kitchen equipment. Ask when the built-in gadgets were installed and try out every item including the oven, washing machine, dryer, etc. Turn on the air-conditioners and listen: some old ones are very noisy.

Malaysia's climate is the ideal breeding environment for fungi and insects. Look in the cupboards, under the sinks and hand-basins, all kitchen and bedroom closets, lift a corner of the wall-to-wall carpet in quest of scurrying beetles. There is no known method of keeping a house entirely bug-free, except by poisoning everything to such an extent that you wouldn't want to live in it yourself. Some houses are less badly infested than others. If you think the place is otherwise all right but too teeming with wildlife, ask for it to be fumigated before you move in. An owner keen to have good tenants will comply with such a request.

An expatriate couple who have successfully survived seven

intercontinental relocations in the last 11 years offer the following advice to house-hunters: "Look At Three More."

After you have found a house that you think will suit you, look at three more. If none of these three is as good as your first choice, you have found a house that you will be reasonably satisfied with. Very often, the supernumerary One, Two or Three is superior to the first choice.

## HOUSEHOLD HELP AVAILABLE

It is a commonly accepted fact that no foreign woman can keep house unaided below the Tropic of Cancer. European or Asian, if she's not Malaysian she can't sweep or cook or wash windows or scrub bathrooms. She needs a servant, preferably servants, to do all these things for her.

The origins of this myth are unclear; the Empire may have helped to nurse it in India. In that wonderful place, so we learn, one had to employ an army of servants to do their own thing each. The one who could empty chamber pots was incapable of grooming the master's horse. No way could the cook also carry a tea tray into the verandah. Given strict hierarchy even in the servants' quarters, it becomes clear that the memsahib herself could not possibly have emptied chamber pots, groomed a horse, made tea or carried a tray anywhere at all.

Them were the days!

In the 1990s, matters are a little different. It is perfectly possible for a healthy grown-up woman of whatever race to keep house in Malaysia. Indoor plumbing and motorcars dispense with the chamber pot and stable chores. Household machinery is available, as are cleaning services and laundromats. Lots of Malaysian mothers do all the housework themselves, with mimimum help from dad and the kids, and often hold down a part-time or full-time job as well.

The expatriate sole-charge housewife is not the norm, however. The majority of foreign households employ at least one servant, many two or three.

Some expatriate wives have not had household help before, and are nervous about directing somebody else — a stranger! — to do what they secretly feel is their bounden duty. Mrs Beeton rises up to haunt the best of us at times, but there is no need for a guilt complex on this subject.

A competent worker offers to do your household chores in return for adequate payment. You are helping her to earn an income which she needs, and which you can afford to pay. Once you have worked out a routine between the two of you, you will have time to do all the things you always wanted to but never could because housework tied you to the sink all day.

Servants are available in Malaysia, and, provided helper and housewife hit it off together, they are a boon. Variously known as "amah", "helper", "servant" or "maid", they vary in age from school leavers to middle-aged women. The best household helper is obviously one who has worked before, and who comes well recommended from her former employer. Young girls should only be employed if the mistress spends a lot of her time at home and will be able to supervise and train the maid, or if there is a senior servant to show her the ropes.

## What Can a Domestic Worker be Expected to Do?

**Housekeeper:** This is the highest-paid domestic position. An experienced housekeeper can be trusted with the running of the entire household. The mistress can ring her up at 5 p.m. with the message that there will be guests for dinner, briefly outline the desired menu, and leave her to do the rest. The dinner will be served at the appointed time, with all the linen and silver in place and the right wines in the cooler.

A housekeeper is never the only servant in a house. In consultation with the housewife, she hires and fires subsidiary helpers. She may also keep a sharp eye on gardeners and drivers. A bit of a dragon, a competent housekeeper's price is above rubies — spoil her if you have one, or risk having her lured away by Lady Smythe-Jones down the road!

**Cook:** The cook's job is to cook. Depending on her previous employers and training, she may be proficient in a number of different cuisines. She will not look after the children and walk the dog and polish the floors — that's what you keep servants for! She usually does the shopping, and keeps provisions stocked in the freezer and the store cupboards. She should be able to, or learn to, bake homemade bread and make pickles and preserves.

There used to be a male "cookie", who padded about barefoot in Somerset Maugham stories. Smooth and basically dishonest, he served endless curry tiffins to planters too sloshed in gin to appreciate them, but he is practically extinct. The overwhelming majority of today's cooks are female.

**General servant:** She is the one you are most likely to employ, the woman who helps with the cleaning and cooking and child-minding but needs supervision by the resident housewife. Depending on where she has worked before, she is a "good plain cook", but if you want her to prepare your own special dishes you will have to train her.

The general servant cannot be expected to keep house unaided. It is a matter of personal choice how tasks are divided; some mothers prefer to attend to their children themselves. Cleaning, washing and ironing is nearly always done by the maid.

It is a good idea to work out a house-cleaning system. Each floor needs to be mopped or polished (depending on what it is made of) once a week, the kitchen probably twice. Sinks, bathrooms and basins need a daily wipe and a weekly scrub. Mattresses, pillows and other bedding should be aired in the sun once a week to keep out the musty smell our damp climate promotes. A room roster ensures that windows get washed once a month, cupboards and wardrobes are turned out once a quarter.

Regular cleaning of this kind reduces the need for a proper "spring-clean", which is very strenuous business in a tropical climate! If a system is adhered to, the servant can be expected to keep it up even if the family is absent for a few days, or the mistress is away on holiday.

For the first couple of weeks, the mistress has to be at home most of the time to "show and tell" her servant how she likes the household run. There's no point in giving her a two-hour lecture on the first day. She won't remember even half of it; under the circumstances neither would you. Tell her, every day until she has got into a routine, how you want things done. Show her how to handle household machines. If she is not familiar with them, show her several times, and carefully supervise her first few attempts. This is in both your interests — it gives her confidence, and it preserves your valuable appliances!

If the amah has much to do with the children, be sure you agree on how they are to be disciplined, what standard of manners, etc, you want to enforce. The helper is likely to be "soft", especially with babies and toddlers. Malaysian children are petted and humoured while they are small. A crying baby is carried by grannies, aunties and sisters in turn. A toddler can arrange to have his own way by throwing well-timed tantrums. The whole family will do anything to prevent or stop a small child from crying; if this is not the way you want your children brought up, make it very clear to your servant.

Make it equally clear to both your servant and your children that they will not be allowed to boss her (the servant) around and ask her to perform tasks which they can do for themselves. If you have decided that your teenage children will clean their own rooms every morning, for instance, make enough personal inspections to be sure they are really doing their chores and not just passing them on to Ah Moy!

In some families this situation arises without the mother noticing. The servant gets sullen and seems not to like the children as enthusiastically as she did at the start, but she would never complain to her employer.

Japanese women in Malaysia have their own network of servants, passed from one family to another as the husband's stint of work here is over. Many of these girls have picked up a certain amount of Japanese from their employers. They have learnt the Japanese household routine, and — most important! — they have mastered some simple Japanese cooking.

Such girls are handed down from one Japanese family to another; this is by far the best way to find a good servant. The newcomer to Malaysia is well advised to plug into her compatriots' local network as soon as possible, and try to find a servant by recommendation.

This is always the big question: where and how to find a good servant? To find just any servant is easy; the expatriate is the preferred employer.

### Finding the Right Maid

There is no foolproof way. The following suggestions have been made by a large number of foreign women and a few men, but the bottom line is: Even the best-recommended servant is of no use if you don't get on with her. There is such a thing as immediate liking, or immediate disliking, between persons. The housewife will have the most to do with domestic staff, but her husband and the children have to get on with the helper too. Allow for instinct when it comes to admitting a stranger into your family circle.

1) Ask around your community association. There are a number of these; every newcomer should get in touch with one or more of them. Some associations have a newsletter in which informal advertisements can be placed.

2) Ask friends to consult their own domestic staff, drivers or gardeners as well as household helpers. Sometimes a servant has a

relative or friend who is looking for work. The danger here is that, to please the mistress, a basically unwilling cousin may be pressed into service. The advantage is that your friend's servant is not likely to recommend a totally unsuitable applicant, because he or she would in the end be held responsible for complaints!

3) Ask your "van man", the food vendor who tours your area every morning, or put up a notice in the local shop. These methods are not really recommended to the newcomer who does not yet know her tradesmen.

4) Place an advertisement in the *Malay Mail* (Kuala Lumpur's English-language evening paper) or your local paper. It is usually safer not to publish an address or phone number, but make use of the paper's numbered listings.

5) Consult an employment agency. Most agencies levy a fee, but introduce servants "on consignment": if either party is dissatisfied with the arrangement it can be terminated within 15 days.

## What Qualifications May be Expected of a Domestic Servant?

At the first interview, ensure that you can communicate with her. As she applied to work for an expatriate family, she must speak reasonably fluent English. Carefully read the testimonials from her former employers, ask to see her Identity Card and note down the number. Nobody in Malaysia resents this sort of security check; we are constantly told to produce our IC for some purpose or other!

Have a good look at the photo on the IC and the person who presents it. It has occasionally happened that a girl applied with testimonials and papers borrowed from a sister or friend!

Ask questions about the girl's family. Is she from nearby or from a remote area? Are her parents alive, has she any kinfolk living in your town? You may wish to contact relatives if she should fall ill. If she has lots and lots of phone calls from brothers and boy cousins the employer may wish to confirm with a respectable aunt that the family really is so very numerous and all-male.

It is a good idea to make it clear from the start if you do not wish the girl to use your house as her friends' meeting place, and that you do not wish your phone number distributed to all and sundry. Some employers forbid their maids to use the phone at all. While they are present in the house this restriction can be enforced, not at other times.

If you have small children, ask a prospective amah if she has younger brothers or sisters or if there were children at her last place of employment. It is also of vital importance that she be a person of clean habits and good health if she is going to look after your baby! The second of these qualities can be ascertained by a medical examination. Send her to your family doctor for a thorough check-up. This is a normal procedure which no candidate will resent; of course you pay the doctor's fees.

Ask the girl about her religion, and which major holidays she will require off. It is a good idea to settle these matters at the first interview, to avoid being presented with an impromptu "religious holiday" almost every month in future!

Malay girls should be given a week off at Hari Raya, Chinese girls at Chinese New Year or Christmas, Indian girls at Deepavali or Christmas, Borneo natives at Gawai Dayak (or Harvest Festival) as the case may be. Besides this, a day off a week or a whole weekend each fortnight is a reasonable amount of free time.

A Muslim servant will not handle food that contains pork in any form. Even if the housewife does the cooking, she may decline to wash dishes on which pork has been served. She won't be happy if there is a dog on the premises, she will certainly not bathe it. It is indeed possible to provide a servant with socks, gloves, tongs and the like to avoid contamination, but it doesn't make for work efficiency! A family that eats pork regularly and keeps dogs should not employ Muslim helpers.

## *Employing a Maid*

Expatriates pay higher wages than local employers do, and generally expect shorter working hours of their maids. There is no law regulating minimum wages or maximum hours in Malaysia. There is not even a universal sickness insurance. The domestic employee is at the mercy of her boss.

Servants can be enrolled with the Employees Provident Fund, a version of old-age insurance. This is not compulsory. There is no national pension scheme in Malaysia. EPF monies are invested, and each contributor receives a lump payment of all her contributions plus interest when she reaches the age of 55.

Employer and employee pay 11 per cent and 9 per cent respectively of the monthly EPF contribution. It does not amount to very much, but it will mean a lot to your servant when she reaches late middle age!The above information applies to local staff. In the last few years it has become possible to recruit Filipino maids in Malaysia. The Immigration and Labour Departments get into this, with the attendant red tape and delays.

The prospective employer of a Filipina has to be married, his wife and children residing with him. He has to have a Malaysian work permit of at least two years' duration. The application has to be supported by a sheaf of documents not omitting copies of the employer's personal documents, photos of himself, wife and children. He has to pay the maid's air passage to and from the Philipines, and a number of other levies.

Many employers are prepared to put up with all the fuss and the three-month waiting period to recruit a Filipina. They are usually good if inexperienced workers, affectionate with children, and obviously not going to rush "home to mother" at a minute's notice, the way some local servants are inclined to do.

The exact terms and conditions of applying for a Filipino servant change from time to time. Up-to-date details are available from the Immigration Department (KL 255 5027, 257 8155).

41

## *Three Commonly Faced Problems*

The three main problems foreign employers seem to encounter with domestic staff are a) honesty, b) discretion, and c) the maids' private lives.

a) Unfortunately, there is no universal formula for dealing with this. Most maids are honest. Some are honest if they are not tempted with valuables lying around the house. A very few are dishonest.

Please do not accuse your servant of stealing if something in the house has gone missing unless you are absolutely sure! The item may have been mislaid, or taken by a family member who did not think of telling you. Inform the family, very publicly, that something is missing; sometimes such an article is quite miraculously found again half an hour later. If this kind of miracle becomes too frequent, and you are sure none of your children are responsible, you may have to consider looking for a new servant.

b) Can a person stop her maid from gossiping about her family's private concerns? She can't. In all fairness it must be admitted that much time is spent by women at morning teas talking about their servants, too. Only we don't call that gossip...

A maid is not supposed to discuss her employer's lives with others, of course. She should be informed of this at the time she is first employed. On the other hand, the Victorian warning: "Never Quarrel in Front of the Servants" still holds good in the 20th century. The temptation to gossip is small if there is nothing much to gossip about; nobody could base a series of titillating revelations on your breakfast menus, favourite TV programmes and choice of car polish.

c) The maid's private life concerns you as little as yours concerns her. In other words: how can you avoid noticing it, living at close quarters the way you do? But you have to ignore it as much as possible.

Quite a number of domestic workers are married. Her family may live in your "amah quarters", in which case you must firmly refuse to referee every disagreement between her and her husband or children. Advise her to call the police if she complains of physical ill-treatment.

If you consider employing a married woman, discuss the possibility of a pregnancy. Should she get pregnant, up to what time will she work? How much time will she require off? Where will she live during her confinement period? Will she help you find a temporary replacement for the duration?

A single helper is likely to have phone calls and boy friends. She will go out on dates or entertain friends in her room. Make your views clear at a very early stage; do you want her to bring people to the house? If yes, only girl friends? Up to what hour, how often? If the girl is very young, some discussion with her mother or other relatives may be a good idea.

No, you are not responsible for maintaining another family's moral standards. But neither do you want to be blamed for an unwanted entanglement (or pregnancy) if things go wrong.

## DOING WITHOUT

It is indeed possible to manage a household without help. The house you rent almost certainly has a washing machine installed; if not, they are available here in a great variety of choices. The Laundromat is making an appearance in the shopping centres of residential areas, catering mostly for working bachelors of both genders whose families live "outstation" as the country areas are called. Nothing prevents an expatriate from using them, however.

There are cleaning services in town which will wash windows, polish floors, or do all the domestic cleaning including cupboards. These may be engaged on a regular basis, or only for the occasional spring-clean. Grass cutting and drain cleaning are also undertaken by contractors, if you prefer not to employ a gardener.

A number of expatriate wives are doing it all with their own two hands. Some young couples, especially if they do not yet have a family, prefer a little privacy. They may get windows washed and floors polished by a cleaning service, but otherwise the young wife, who has no outside employment anyway, is in sole charge.

The Yellow Pages of the phone book list the necessary services that should make Life Without Amahs not only possible but actually comfortable for a single person or childless couple. Even young mothers have been known to manage on their own, though most prefer the convenience of a live-in baby-sitter.

## WHAT TO BRING FROM HOME

Some expatriates bring their household lock, stock, and barrel, when they move overseas. Others bring nothing at all except what they can carry in their suitcases. Most fall between these two extremes.

People who come here to work with big companies usually have a fully furnished house put at their disposal. They may bring silver and china, ornaments to decorate the house to their own taste.

Furniture, household machinery, household utensils of good quality are available in Malaysia. Before shipping in valuable furniture, especially if it is antique, consider how well it will stand the transport and the rather damp climate. It should also be remembered that the household current in Malaysia is 220/240; transformers would therefore be needed to run your electrical equipment here.

Most hobby supplies are available in the big towns, including a wide range of artists' materials in specialist shops. Home dressmakers will be entranced by the wide choice of dress materials, but she needs to bring her own patterns because few are sold here. Generously built women are advised to bring foundation garments from their home country — the C-cup is the biggest fitting found anywhere in KL. Even in Singapore, the usual resort for specialized shopping, the D-cup is a practically unknown quantity. Some salesgirls primly aver that there is No Such Thing!

This warning applies to really big shoe sizes, both for men and women. It is possible to get shoes custom-made in the bigger centres, but the styling and standard of workmanship may not be to a foreign buyer's taste. Clothes of any size can be made by local tailors and dressmakers.

Malaysian dressmakers and tailors are very efficient and, by world standards, inexpensive. A new arrival is usually introduced to one by a friend. It is a good idea to order a simple garment first and see how it turns out. If even two or three fittings don't produce quite the right result, shop around for another craftsperson. You will eventually find one who's just right.

Most dressmakers work from pictures or rough drawings. The customer can bring an illustration cut from a fashion magazine and request a dress "just like this one", or "with only one row of buttonholes" or whatever. Most dressmakers prefer taking measurements for each new garment they make; the occasional very shy local woman brings along her blouse or jacket as a pattern and demands the new item be made "just this size". With loose styles like the *baju kurung*, this method seems to work!

Many dress shops sell good quality off-the-rack clothing. Women often make use of this opportunity to replenish their wardrobes. There are no standard sizes; S, M and L can mean anything at all, and there are mountains of "free-size" blouses and shifts around. "Fit anybody!" a 1.47m salesgirl assures a 1.8m shopper. Does she really think the same shirt would fit her and this customer?

There is no need to bring any really warm clothes to Malaysia. A man will need one or serveral suits, depending on whether he needs to wear one to work, and a good supply of casual clothes for leisure and sportswear. A woman needs lots and lots of summer frocks, from plain and sensible to really pretty because they will often double as outdoor party clothes. A few warmish items are required for functions which take place in air-conditioned rooms. I have arctic memories of public assembly halls where my teeth chattered all the way through concert and ballet performances...

Party and evening dresses should be lovely, glittery, colourful and demure. Bare backs, plunging necklines, bodices without visible means of support, are considered immodest. Nobody will throw an "indecently" attired woman out of a party, but she will be quietly indexed as "loose" by all who saw her. This goes for very, very short skirts or shorts in the daytime, halter tops, or clinging tops worn without undergarments. It is quite possible that the sight of a statuesque blonde plop-plop-plopping her way down the bazaar entertains the loungers there, but her shameless appearance will also reconfirm local suspicions about the general immorality of foreigners.

## MONEY MATTERS

The Malaysian banking system is, on the whole, similar to the British. If you make out a cheque that the recipient will need to cash, do not cross it!

For some odd reason, quite a number of shops are reluctant to accept a personal cheque in payment.

A few shopkeepers add a percentage of "commission" to goods paid for by credit card. They are of course not supposed to do such a thing. If you politely request the use of a telephone to call the credit card company in question, the price may suddenly sink down to normal again. If not, ask for a detailed receipt clearly stating the list price, and the augmented price, and contact your card company with a formal complaint.

Foreigners who plan to stay in Malaysia for any length of time should consider opening an account with the National Savings Bank. This is the bank with the most branches in the country — every Post Office is also an agent for basic transactions. If you go travelling, you need not carry very much cash because you can draw on any branch of the NSB (Bank Simpanan Nasional); in Post Offices there is a withdrawal limit of $400, not to be repeated within ten days.

This is only relevant if you travel "outstation", to rural or remote areas. In towns and district centres, the more common credit cards are accepted by the larger shops and hotels.

## DRIVING AND YOU

Should you, or shouldn't you, drive a car in Malaysia?

There is no good reason against it. By law, you need to have a valid driver's licence from your own country. As a wise precaution, familiarize yourself with the Malaysian Road Code first. The road signs look the same, but text on them is usually printed only in Bahasa Malaysia.

A foreigner can drive here for three months with an International Driver's Licence or his own country's licence, then he has to apply for a local one. If the original licence is in a language other than English, Bahasa Indonesia or Mandarin, it has to be translated and witnessed at the local Embassy before it is presented at the Road Transport Department here. There is no restriction on who may drive, provided the person is over 18 years of age, physically fit and of sound mind.

The question arises, from time to time, whether the other guys on the road are of sound mind. During a recent police operation to catch wayward bus drivers, a plainclothes cop who travelled as a passenger counted 12 traffic law violations during a one-hour trip. When he stopped the demon-driver and booked him, the man got abusive — a rate of one misdemeanour per five minutes seemed an acceptable average, and what the hell was all the fuss about?

Malaysians are a forward-looking people. This otherwise admirable trait seems to prevent many of them from looking in a rear-vision mirror, ever. The car in front of you may do anything, with no reference whatever to the fact that you exist and are right there, driving at a normal cruising speed, four and a half metres behind it. Be warned! Keep your distance! Don't get unduly startled at being

overtaken from left, right or elsewhere by motorbikes. They're forward-looking too...

Once in a while you will come across a car, awkwardly parked, that's sprouting greenery from the rear. The climate is not at fault, nor is the driver a person of strong ecological principle; the car is simply out of order. The red Emergency Triangle is not commonly known here.

Remember it in case your car plays up: if you don't have a Triangle, stick a twig from a roadside bush in the rear fender to notify other drivers that your vehicle is out of commission. Leaving the boot open and the emergency blinkers on will also convey the message, but this isn't practical if the car has to be left there for hours.

Should you be involved in a minor accident, you have the option to "settle out of court" if both parties agree to this. The law obliges you to report within 24 hours an accident that caused major material damage or severe injury to a person. If an accident is to be reported, do not move any vehicles or injured person (unless it is necessary for first aid) until the police arrive.

You may be unlucky enough to have hit, or been hit by, an uncouth character who gets noisily abusive or threatens violence. Such cases are rare, but they do exist. As a precaution, lock the doors and stay in your car (if this is compatible with safety) until the police arrive; ask a bystander to call 999 for you. There will be no shortage of bystanders at the scene of an accident involving an expatriate, especially if she be female!

If you have hurt somebody, of course you make every effort to get the person to hospital. One word of caution: in the more remote rural areas, it can happen that villagers gang up on and attack a motorist who has hit one of their group. This is not the norm, in fact it's extremely unusual, but it can happen. If you feel threatened, don't stop and attempt to discuss the matter. Proceed as fast as possible to the nearest police station, hospital, or any place out of reach of the angry crowd from where you can make a report by telephone, and summon the necessary help.

Where the cadaver lies, vultures gather. Where there is a road accident in Malaysia, tow trucks appear as if from nowhere. Angry drivers charge that a few "road-hogs" are actually paid by fly-by-night panelbeating firms to cause accidents, conveniently within crashing distance from the workshop, to keep up the GNP. No such charges have been proved to date, but the fact remains that the tow trucks often reach the scene of an accident before the Ambulance or the Police!

Drivers are advised to note the number, colour and relevant details of a car that deliberately caused an accident (by abrupt braking without cause, for instance, so the car behind crashed into you) and then sped off.

The tow truck attendants offer to help. If a confused, upset accident victim only half-nods his head, he has a bit of paper shoved under his nose, a pen pressed into his hand to scrawl a signature.

Then he sees his car pulled up on a hook and towed out of sight. Efficient, prompt and helpful.

The driver recovers his car after a complete engine overhaul (which it didn't need), replaced brake disks, clutch lining and seat covers (which it didn't need), completely re-wired (which it didn't need), and the little dent in the fender elegantly hammered out and re-plated. Chances are that an insurance will refuse to pay even for the accident-related repair if their man didn't inspect the vehicle and assess the damage before the "helpful" workshop had got its greasy clutches on it.

It is difficult to remain cool, calm and collected after an accident, especially if people are hurt. As a precaution, it is a good idea to carry the phone number of your spouse (office and contact numbers), family doctor and your usual repair shop in the car; taped inside the glovebox is a good place. Don't permit any tow truck man to touch the vehicle. Do not sign any papers until you have made a police report and your insurance company has inspected the damage.

Cars do not need a Warrant of Fitness in Malaysia. They must be insured at least for third-party risk, the Road Tax cannot be renewed unless a valid insurance certificate is produced. The road tax receipt is a circular sticker that has to be displayed on the windscreen at all times. Driving without either the road tax disc or a valid licence, with damaged or fancily lettered licence plates, with defective lights and blinkers, is worth a fine in Malaysia just like everywhere else.

It is illegal for your car and my car to have dark windows; a passenger sedan of up to 2000 cc can be stopped and penalized for the offence on the grounds that opaque monsters on the road endanger traffic. They do too. If the opaque car is huge and new, on the other hand, or if it has a Z licence plate, it vrooms on without let or hindrance. Drivers who understand about relativity suspect Einstein had a hand in this...

## MAN'S BEST FRIEND

"Don't kiss the cat!" a little Australian girl warns a visitor who's getting unnecessarily friendly with the resident feline, "she's got germs."

This child's mother obviously has a very uncaring attitude towards her daughter's relationship with pets ... on the other hand, this child is mercifully free from ringworm, ticks, worms, stomach upsets and other unpleasant conditions people can, and do, pick up from domestic animals in the tropics.

*Rule 1* in the acquisition and keeping of pets: Is the animal healthy? and can we keep it healthy?

Children from time to time find a pitifully whimpering puppy or kitten somewhere; the garden of a foreign family is a favourite dumping ground for unwanted animals. Have such a foundling carefully checked by a vet, and make no promise about keeping it until his verdict is in. Children have got to learn that one part of being kind to animals may consist in not adopting them, but having them put painlessly out of an incurable misery.

Think twice before bringing a family pet from overseas to Malaysia. To start with, there are quarantine regulations. Animals from countries other than Australia, New Zealand, Great Britain, Ireland and Singapore will be detained for four weeks or longer at the discretion of the veterinary officer at Subang Airport. They need to have valid vaccination certificates and health papers in all cases; they will generally be vaccinated against rabies again upon their arrival at the Subang Quarantine Station.

Depending on your country of origin, your pet may find the climate hard to adjust to. Many imported animals succumb to diseases they have no resistance to because they have not been exposed to them before; tick fever is one example. From time to time the population of stray dogs in Malaysia's larger towns are decimated by an epidemic of canine distemper which can spread rapidly to even the best-behaved domestic pooch.

A locally-bred pet is fully acclimatized. While there is much to be said in favour of thoroughbreds, especially dogs, they are more delicate and temperamental. As a family pet and for barking purposes, the local "town terrier" is not a bad choice. Friends whose dog has just had a litter will be only too pleased to offer you a puppy — or two puppies — or three puppies!

Dogs need to be licenced if you live in a town area; this law alas is observed more in the breach than the observance. Get your dog's tag from the town hall or the Municipal Health Department, and let's hope you start a trend.

Dogs need to be regularly washed, a chore carried out by the gardener in many households. Another rather unpleasant job goes with dog-shampooing: ticks have to be picked off the animal's body and destroyed. This is to prevent them from multiplying. If you intend to keep a dog, mention this when you interview a prospective gardener. If he is Muslim, he may decline to touch any canine. This means you'll have to persuade the amah to give Rover his weekly shampoo, or do it yourself.

Most Muslims object to being touched by a dog. Do not take your pet with you when you go visiting people's houses, however impeccable its social manners. If Muslims come to visit you, chain Rover up. Your assurance that he doesn't bite is beside the point. The dog's friendly lick is considered defiling, and may upset your Malay friends. Do not offer your hand for a shake if you have just been patting the dog; wash it first.

If you plan to take your pet travelling with you, check in advance that your hotel will give it house-room. Don't be too disappointed if they say NO; it is not customary in Malaysia for dogs, cats or other pets to stay in hotels with their owners. If your servant can't cope with them in your absence, there are resident kennels in the bigger towns.

It is advisable that female dogs be spayed. There are quite enough canines in Malaysia at the present moment without a new litter of puppies in every back garden! Think of the future, too; when your stint in the country is up and you have to dispose of your pets, a spayed bitch is much easier to find a new home for than a merrily reproducing one.

## WORK PERMIT AND THE WORKING WIFE

Malaysian labour laws are bad news to the foreign working woman. She has been pursuing her own career ever since the children grew out of their nappies; in Malaysia she needs to apply for a work permit to take on so much as a typist's job — and she very likely won't get it. There are hundreds of unemployed typists around.

Many contract work agreements specifically forbid the officer's spouse from taking on paid employment in Malaysia. If no such prohibition is expressed, a foreigner looking for work here still needs a work permit, in most cases difficult to get. Some women can fill their hours with sports, Malay lessons, household, charities and hobbies. Others have found a little way around the legal barrier.

There are many very rewarding occupations in the creative field. You don't need a work permit for writing, painting, photographing, giving tuition in all manner of things from artistic cake decoration to English, French, Japanese or German for Beginners. Many foreign women earn a little pin money by this sort of occupations.

One of the first things you should do if you come here to settle is to contact your community's association. In KL there are American, Australian, British, Japanese and other clubs which you can contact through your Embassy or High Commisison. Through these groups you can find out who else shares your tastes and hobbies, your ideas or problems. Their members are people who have resided here longer than you have and can give you a few pointers. There is no need to be reluctant or ashamed to take advice; in six month's time, you'll be the "old hand" dispensing counsel to new arrivals!

## OF GHOSTIES AND GHOULIES

*"Hantu! hantu!"* a hysterical voice screams from the kitchen; if you're lucky the neighbours' amahs will hear it too and come running across to join in the fun. *Hantu* is a ghost or ghosts; they are likely to reduce their female spectators to screaming hysteria and that condition is very contagious. *Hantu* have a sneaky way of turning up where least expected or welcome.

Maybe the last word needs qualification. *Hantu* turn up wherever they have an appreciative audience. If you simply don't believe in spooks you'll never meet one. But if your amah, your gardener or your driver is on that sort of wavelength, he or more usually she will "hear something" or "see something" at the most inconvenient moment possible.

Normally, ghosties and ghoulies leave expats alone. You can have interesting discussions about the supernatural with your local friends, all of whom aver that of course they don't believe in those things — but the neighbourhood *bomoh,* temple medium, soothsayer and astrologer all do good business.

There is a wide range of local superstition, all very interesting in its way. Pointing at a rainbow will make your finger drop off; a girl who sings in the kitchen is fated to marry an old man; if cats are allowed to jump over a corpse it will sit up as a ghoul; the dead with a grievance can appear to the living, so never give a lift to an unknown hitchhiker near a graveyard; a woman who died in childbirth turns into a horrible monster out to revenge herself on men; if a kitchen utensil has been dropped three times it must be left on the floor because a ghost wants it; a crab that has managed to pincer somebody's finger or toe will hang on until it hears thunder; a drop of blood, a strand of hair, a trace of saliva, even a photo can be used to charm its unwitting owner into unwilling love of the person who has possession of any of the above. The list is endless; superstitions can be a very interesting conversation topic among friends who will be curious to hear what you have to say about walking under ladders and keeping umbrellas open indoors.

Ghost stories are an accepted way of making children timid and docile, too frightened to move very far away from their adult protector. In the villages, children aren't supposed to go outside the house at night — neither will they if granny's stories about Things that Lurk in the Dark are scary enough.

If your young children are suddenly frightened of the dark or can't be left alone any more, check what sort of stories Timah has been telling them. Have a word with her, privately, making it quite clear to her that your children don't need this kind of education. It is also a good idea if you put them to bed yourself whenever possible, for it is at bedtime that the ghosties flourish. The Late Night Horror Show has the same effect here that it has on sensitive minds the world over: horror-struck spectators sit frozen to their armchairs and don't dare go to bed because it would involve turning off the lights...

There may be a problem if for some reason your domestic staff decide that your house is haunted. It has on occasion happened that a house with such a reputation is rented to expatriates because they wouldn't have heard the off-putting gossip. Neighbouring amahs will waste no time telling your girl that a headless white woman or an indigo man is to be seen prowling the grounds on the night of the full moon. The story nearly always starts with: "During the Japanese occupation..." and ends with a murder or suicide. Then it depends on the hearer's common sense and her "strength of soul" as the ability to resist the supernatural is called in Malay.

She may weigh the certain advantages of a good job with friendly employers against the theoretical possibility of meeting a white woman or a blue man, and simply keep her curtains tightly shut on the nights of the full moon. Or she will start to look out for the visitations. If she does this in the right spirit she'll see them soon enough.

Telling a hysterical person to "snap out of it!" is useless. Once she has lost control, she cannot. She is convinced that she is in the grip of whatever she thinks she saw, or heard her friends say they saw.

The immediate treatment is to prevent the patient from harming herself, and let her have her scream out. After a while she will calm down and "wake up". Make a cup of tea, soothe her as best you can, assure her that nobody else "saw" anything at all and that she may simply have had a bad dream.

Next day, have a talk with the girl. Tell her that if she feels there is a supernatural threat in the house, she should resign and permit you to look for another servant. It may be what she secretly hoped for. Mass hysteria occurs where large numbers of females are penned together under uncongenial circumstances, as in nurses' homes, school hostels and factories, and it breaks out at times of stress like exams. You are giving the girl a face-saving way of leaving a job she is for some reason unhappy in. Maybe she's homesick.

On the other hand, would she like to go home for a day or so, and come back after her family have said special prayers for her or administered such other consolation as seems suitable? This is a once-only chance, of course — don't make ghosts an occasion for extra holidays whenever desired! This solution is face-saving too; it permits her to discuss with her parents whether she wants to continue working with you (and the potential ghost) or not.

A firm, friendly handling should defuse most *hantu* situations. Don't ridicule the person's fears. Don't tell her she's imagining it all, it's stupid to believe in ghosts, she's making it up to get an extra holiday, etc. This is insensitive; the person affected does believe she saw and heard things. As far as she is concerned you are simply talking brashly about things you don't understand. And so you may be!

In the unlikely situation that several of your staff see and hear things, frequently, you may have to call in competent aid to cleanse the premises. Depending on your religious beliefs, this can be tricky. Christians call in a priest or pastor to say prayers, sprinkle Holy Water, etc — but what if your staff are Moslem? In that case, you should call on a locally recommended bomoh. If your staff are Chinese, a temple medium or a Buddhist monk is indicated.

Some expatriates may consider it entertaining or at least exciting to have an exorcism performed in their own house (it will also be somewhat expensive). Others feel outraged. It's all a matter of viewpoints. Parents are concerned about the impression this sort of mumbo-jumbo will make on innocent young minds.

It may be better to pack the children off on an impromptu "holiday" with friends. Let them spend a night or two away from home while the ghosts, *hantu* and ghoulies are laid to rest once and for all by a competent professional.

## THE COST OF AIR AND OTHER INTERESTING ITEMS

Do not get flustered when you get your first "Air" Bill. In places like downtown KL the air is of such a quality that inhabitants should be subsidized for consenting to breathe it, and here's a bill for the smog ... well no, what you're holding is a water bill. Pronounced "ayer", it means water. The other bills you get every month are for power and the telephone.

These bills can be paid at Post Offices, the SBBS (one-stop payment centres) in many shopping complexes and public buildings, the National Savings Bank if you have a giro account, at the main offices of the Water Board, the Power Board (Lembaga Letrik Negara) and the Syarikat Telekom Malaysia (the Telephone company, STM). A number of commercial banks have arrangements which permit the public to pay utility bills by bank card.

Power and water cuts occur in all parts of the world, they occur here. One reason for reading the local daily is that interruptions for public works are announced in the press. This helps you to plan your day without power, to fill buckets and tubs with water in advance.

In the case of unscheduled breaks, ring the local power board or water board.

You should have a list of useful numbers right next to the phone — the emergency call for ambulance, police and fire brigade in towns is 999 and 994, in districts it may be different. Find out at your leisure so you have them handy if anything happens. Spend half an hour with the phone book; consult a friend who can help you decipher its mysteries. Government offices and statutory bodies are listed in a separate section, which is compiled in Bahasa Malaysia; an index at the front gives the official translations. With all this help, it can be quite difficult to guess what a certain office or department might be listed under. Don't wait until something has gone wrong before starting to flip-flip-flip through the hefty volume in feverish haste.

It is useful to have the City Hall or Municipal Council number handy in case you need to complain about slack services, blocked drains, a dead dog on the road, a stray cow or buffalo in the garden, a python in the downstairs bathroom. You'll need your grocer's number, your neighbours' in case strange noises are heard at night, the local hospital and your doctor's.

# Chapter Four

# THE MALAYSIAN LANGUAGES

The official language of Malaysia is Bahasa Melayu, literally "Malay Language", a standardized form of Malay. Many people know English quite well, another lot know some English, but if you plan to stay here for any length of time you should make an effort to learn at least basic Malay.

Malay is the common language of Malaysia, but by no means the only one. Four and a half million Chinese speak their various dialects and in most cases some Mandarin; one and a half million Indians speak various languages of the Indian subcontinent. Should you travel to East Malaysia, thirty or more native dialects are

*A shopping centre displays the traditional Christmas greeting in Bahasa Melayu.*

spoken in the two States of Sarawak and Sabah. But nearly all these peoples know at least a little Malay. It may be the pidgin form, known as "bazaar Malay" which is understood from the southern Philippines to as far as Sumatra, long known and valued as the lingua franca of the Insulindies.

How does a foreigner set about learning Bahasa Melayu? In a town of any size, there is no difficulty. One may choose between classes or reading with a private tutor; find out if your firm provides language classes for new staff, or staff wives. A variety of books of the teach-yourself kind are available too. Most radio stations have a Learn-a-Word-a-Day programme, often in the early morning so people driving to work can listen in.

Malay vowels are pronounced like Italian, with their full phonetic value.

**a**  as in father
**e**  as in pet
**i**  as in pit
**o**  as in pot
**u**  as in put

There are two trick consonants, a plosive and a liquid. The sound "ch" as in "chicken" is spelt "c". The sound "sh" as in "shut" is spelled "sy". "Syarikat" is pronounced "sharikat"; c-a-t doesn't spell "cat" in Bahasa Melayu, but "chutt", meaning "paint."

If you decide to learn Bahasa Melayu from a book, make sure it is quite new. The language is in a continual process of being enriched and improved, and these laudable efforts don't spare the spelling. What was prefixed ten years ago is hyphenated now, what was elided is now spelled in full. The vocabulary is being manufactured from a variety of sources: do *bengkel* and *sijil* look familiar to any Dutch reader, or the signs *woksyop, kaunter* and *stesyen* to anyone who knows English? My favourite is a signal by the track near Kuala Lumpur's railway station which instructs the train   engineer to "WISEL."

None of these lexical blooms will be found in a Malay book printed in the fifties or sixties. Be sure your grammar and reader are up to date before you embark on self-study.

## *TRY A LITTLE BAHASA MELAYU*

The obvious way to start in a language you hardly know is with small talk. Learned disputes comparing Confucius with Nietzsche come later!

The commonest greeting is:

*Selamat pagi, selamat tengahari* (not so common) or *selamat malam.*

This means "peaceful morning, peaceful noontide, peaceful

evening/night", it is slightly formal, used by a newcomer who is joining a group. Each is answered by the same phrase.

More informal is *Apa khabar?*, What news? This requires a short answer describing the news, or simply *baik, baik!* Everything's fine!

*Nama saya Jenny — apa nama anda?* is next; "My name is Jenny — what's yours?"

The thorny question of personal pronouns comes up very early in your struggle to master Malay. There are several for the second person, formal, informal, respectful or condescending; as an outsider you generally use *anda*. But Malaysians avoid the use of "you" if possible.

Jenny should have said: *Nama saya Jenny — apa nama puan?* "My name is Jenny — what's the lady's name?" *Apa nama tuan* is used for talking to an older man, *apa nama encik?* if addressing a young man. A distinction between older (or married) woman, *puan*, and a younger one, *cik*, is beginning to fade as more young women take their place in the nation's life. *Cik* has something of a Victorian flavour, the sheltered young Miss who waited at home till her parents arranged a marriage for her.

Malaysians in turn will often call her *mem* if she's married, miss if she's single; a European man is generally addressed as *tuan*. These are neocolonial hangovers to be sure, but they contain that little bit of ceremonious formality that goes down well in Malay speech.

To be really polite, she'll not say "I" either; as the conversation continues she refers to herself as "Jenny", "your younger sister (if the interlocutor is considerably older), "your elder sister" or even "your auntie" if he is younger.

It is common to address Malaysians by their work or status title. This eliminates the problem on whether to call a female teacher *puan* or *cik*, for instance — she is *cikgu* whatever her age and civil status. The village elder is called that, *ketua kampung*; any man who wears a white skullcap has performed the pilgrimage to Makkah and is addressed as "Tuan Haji", a woman "Hajjah".

If the discussion centres on buying a bunch of bananas, *saya, anda* and other shortcuts are permissible. But a polite conversation between a middle-aged woman and a young man, after greetings and names have been exchanged, goes like this :

*Encik berasal dari mana?* (Where is the gentleman from?)

*Saya berasal dari Pulau Penang. Puan berasal dari mana?*
(I'm from Penang. Where is madam from?)

*Makcik berasal dari Johor. Encik sudah pindah-kah?*
(Auntie is from Johor. Is the gentleman already married?)

(blushing) *Belum, belum ... berapa orang anak puan?*
(Not yet, not yet ... how many children does madam have?)

*Makcik ada tiga orang anak.*
(Auntie has three children.)

The question about marital status is commonly asked, especially by an older person. Auntie expressed herself discreetly by asking whether he had "already shifted"; this alludes to the custom of a man moving in with his wife's family, if only for a ceremonial week. Bluntly put the question would be: *Encik sudah berkahwin kah?* The negative answer, regardless of age, is "NOT yet".

It is part of small talk to ask how many children a married person has; here also the polite negative is "NOT yet".

Malaysian women like discussing their and other people's children; it is a topic everyone can join because nieces and nephews "count" while grandchildren count double!

"How many children have you got?" may be phrased: "How many children has madam got?" *Berapa orang anak anda?* or *Berapa orang anak mem?* To be extra-refined, children may be poetically if untruthfully described as "the light of your eyes" — thus *Berapa orang cahaya mata anda?*

"I have four children."

*Anak saya empat orang.*

"Are they boys or girls?"

*Berapa orang lelaki, berapa orang perempuan?*

"They are one boy and three girls."

*Satu lelaki, tiga perempuan.*

"How old are your children?"

*Berapa umur mereka masing masing?*

"Are your children in Malaysia with you?"

*Bersamanya anak mem tinggal di Malaysia?*

"My boy is in Canada, my girls are here. They go to school in Kuala Lumpur. What about you; do you have children?"

*Anak saya yang lelaki di Kanada, yang perempuan ada di sini; mereka sekolah di Kuala Lumpur. Puan ada anak?*

"Auntie has seven children, but they are all grown up."

*Makcik (or saya) ada tujuh anak, sudah besar semua.*

"Do you have grandchildren?"

*Puan ada cucu?*

"Yes, auntie has four grandchildren; they live in Johor."

*"Ya, makcik ada empat cucu. Mereka tinggal di Johor."*

Note that despite constant provocation, the polite younger person doesn't call the elder *makcik*. A middle-aged lady describes herself thus out of ceremonial humility; if the younger uses the word, it sounds condescending. A stranger may use *makcik* to a vegetable seller in a village market; it has the social connotation of "my good woman". The male equivalent is *pakcik,* "uncle".

Once you have learnt a little Malay, you will want to practise it. This can sometimes be difficult. You may find yourself in the ridiculous situation of speaking Malay to someone who persistently answers in English, either because you are both polite, or both eager to practise the language. If you are merely asking for road directions from a stranger, don't bother to argue. If it happens with friends, maybe you could make a little pact: let's speak English today, Malay when next we meet, in turn. That way you'll both benefit.

## ENGLISH —LOCAL USAGES

English has been spoken in the Straits region for about two hundred years. In this time, some local usages have evolved. They are quaint as far as they go, but you've got to be alert for special meanings.

A native Chinese speaker is likely to abbreviate the English language considerably; much use is made, and meaning attached to, the simple auxiliary "can".

"Can ah?" means, can this be done, is this all right, may I do it, depending on the tone of voice and expression of face that accompany the question.

"Cannot!" is obvious; another negative possibility is "How can!" This means, absolutely not! expressing several shades of meaning from disapproval to moral outrage.

"Marry my daughter? How can!" is not expressing doubt about the feasibility of the proposition; it tells the young man where he gets off.

"Can ah," expresses permission, "Also can" permission with some silent reservations: "Well, try it if you must!" (we are no longer discussing marriage proposals here). Another variant is the non-committal but very useful :"See first lah!"

In a bracket with "How can!" is the exasperated: "Where got!" to reject an unreasonable demand. You want ice cream cones in the middle of the jungle? "Where got!"

A negative beloved of all shopkeepers is: "No stock!", pronounced: "Noh sto'!" with a strong glottal stop after the sto'. If you insist, they may inform you that: "Last time go'!", meaning they used to have it, but don't have it now.

"Last time" expresses the past tense generally. "Last time my grandfather live in Penang", "last time I go to Raffles Institution", "Last time food so cheap" all describe something that happened quite some time ago.

The logical extension of "last time" is "next time", namely in the future. "Next time I visit you in England!" means I hope to visit you in England one day, not: "on the next of my frequent visits to the northeast Atlantic I'll drop in."

In many cases, the English word has undergone some mutation. A "f'lim" or "f'lem" is a film, both a film show or a roll of film for your camera; this happened because Malay speakers add an "e" between some consonants, making the work "filem"; in rapid speech the "i" is elided and the "e" stressed.

But don't go into a small-town photo shop asking for film, f'lim or f'lem — what you want there is a kodak, never mind what brand they are offering for sale.

Quite a number of brand names are popularly used to express the article itself: "kogate" is Colgate, but describes any toothpaste at all. Housewives ask for "planta" when they mean margarine of any brand. Sanitary pads have entered bazaar speech as "modis".

Life gets more difficult for the expatriate when his local friends talk "Malenglish", or use the exact translation of a Malay word.

"Let's go for *makan*!" is an invitation to go out for a meal, usually at food stalls. ("makan" means "eat".)

But there's more to eating than that. A brake or clutch is supposed to "eat" in the sense of "engage"; a knife has to "eat" in the sense of "cut".

"This brake doesn't eat! The clutch doesn't eat!" is bad news for the owner of the car, worse if it's combined with a tyre that's got no flowers.

"Flower" in this case is the profile; the tyre is bald and needs to be replaced or it won't "eat" next time you brake on a wet road!

"Flower" is the design or decoration on anything, even the ornamentation in instrument playing — a skilled flautist, for instance, embellishes a plain melody with "flowers" in the form of arpeggios or trills, a dancer adds her own "flowers" to the basic steps of a classical performance.

Young people restraining a member of their group from making a Charlie of himself may reprove him with: "Don't *tunjuk,* you!" — don't show off! or "Don't *lebeh,* you!" —don't overdo it!

Your only resource, until you have picked up enough of this curious lingo yourself, is to ask.

"I beg your pardon?" is understood by most, though the standard is: "Eh? eh?"

Avoid saying: "I beg your pardon!" indignantly, with reproving intent. The person addressed may simply repeat what is just said, instead of taking the hint that he shouldn't have said it.

The same applies to an outraged "Do you mind!"

This could happen in a classroom: a boy is happily chatting to his classmate while the teacher is explaining something at the blackboard. She finally turns on him with a pointed: "Ahmad! Do you MIND!" — "Not at all, ma'am," he replies politely. The boy is not being cheeky (probably...), he simply answered the question put to him.

Your Malaysian friends may find the use of: "Do you mind...?" and other negative questions difficult to understand.

"Do you mind showing me the way?" requires "no" for a positive answer (no, I don't mind), but "yes" for the negative (yes, I mind). It is better to make a simple request: "Please show me the way!"

If you only need the way pointed out, fine. But if you want someone to walk there with you, you have to ask: "Could you send me there, please?"

This applies to taking people somewhere by car too, we "send" them, not "take" them.

"Can I follow you?" is a polite request for a lift; "Would you like to follow me home?" is not an invitation to jog along behind the questioner's car, but to have a ride in it.

"Picking somebody up" is abbreviated to "picking".

"I'll come as soon as I've picked the children" doesn't suggest the speaker is going to a shop to pick a couple of kiddies from the vast selection offered there; she is going to pick them UP at the school gate. She most likely has to "pick them home"; she will pick them up, take them home and then join you.

## *WHAT DO THE MINORITIES SPEAK?*

Malaysia contains about five million Chinese-speaking Chinese. This doesn't mean they understand each other! It never fails to amaze foreigners that Chinese may use English or Malay among each other.

Why don't they speak Chinese?

This is like wondering why a Frenchman, a German and an Italian don't "speak European" to each other. In theory, every educated Chinese speaks and writes Mandarin. In practice, it depends on where he went to school; the English-educated, and among the younger crowd the Malay-educated, usually speak their own family's dialect, orally, plus their school language. This also applies to the Borneo natives of East Malaysia.

The same situation obtains among the Indian community, or should one say communities. Tamil and Hindi are the bigger language groups here, but nearly all the dialects of the subcontinent are represented in Malaysia. Many Indians are not only literate in English but very articulate speakers and writers of the language — some of our most respected journalists are Indian! Like almost everybody else, however, Indians do understand at least a vernacular version of Malay.

This may be the place to note that the earliest writers of the Malay language, the authors of some Malay classics, were ethnic Indians who had settled down here and learnt their adopted language really well. Munshi Abdullah who wrote in the 19th century is one of these Indian-Malay writers, but as the court of Malacca was at least partly Indian, many earlier scribes belonged to this group too.

## *LEARN MANDARIN?*

As the international business world becomes increasingly orientated towards Asia, should a foreign business man learn Mandarin?

In principle, yes of course. Any extra language adds to his armoury in corporate warfare. Not only Chinese and Taiwanese business friends will appreciate his learning, Japanese, while they do not usually speak Mandarin, can read the script. The few Mandarin-speaking foreigners in Malaysia are much respected for their achievement.

There is one little drawback. Mandarin is a very, very difficult language to learn. Not only is the speech complex and subtle, the script is hard to grasp for somebody who has been writing more or less phonetically all his life.

If you can take two years off to do nothing else but study Mandarin, you have a good chance of obtaining a basic command of the language. If you try to do it as a one-hour-a-week hobby, you won't get much beyond *La plume de ma tante* or — The Chinese Have a Word for It — *Ta ko tiau tiau, Siaw mau miau miau* (Big dog woof woof, Small cat mew mew).

— *Chapter Five* —

# WAYS OF SEEING
# — YOU AND THEY

The Dowager Countess of Hindersmithwithin's main objection to the Continent is that so many foreigners live there. Neither her maid nor her footman dare tell the old lady that in Italy or France, *she* is the foreigner...

Even modern, well-adjusted working people in a foreign land need a little time to handle this peculiar feeling that they are the outsiders. They get stared at in the streets, whispered about by shopping housewives and giggled at by schoolgirls, because they look different.

"Like, I mean, I look normal. The other guys are a little brownish-yellow, their eyes are rather narrow and their hair is pitch black..." says a blue-eyed blond. But when in Malaysia, the yellow-brownish guys with the black hair are the norm! Cosmopolitans have less difficulty here than those who come straight from a smallish community in, say, northeastern Switzerland, but it hits us all at different times in different ways.

It is impossible for a foreigner to just blend into the Malaysian landscape. He will be noticed; it is his responsibility to get noticed for all the right reasons.

Malaysians are prepared to be tolerant of an expatriate who tries to behave properly but doesn't quite make it, especially when he's only been here a few years. A general attitude of "he doesn't know any better" protects him from public censure. After some time, when a foreign resident has made some good friends, they will give him a quiet hint about something he's been doing, or saying (his Malay is adequate but he's been addressing his servants wrongly) that isn't quite right.

Remember at all times that the Malaysians you come into contact with, however fleetingly, see you as The Foreigner. They will think of Those Nice Foreigners if you behave acceptably, Those Stupid Foreigners or Those Nasty Foreigners if you do not. Five hundred people see you in the street; that's five hundred opinions influenced to the good, or the bad!

There is the occasional Letter to the Editor in the local Press, lambasting a careless expat driver — "Those Foreigners think they can flout our traffic laws with impunity, and it is high time that something was done..." etc, etc. I have no statistics at hand, but I'd be surprised if one per cent of convicted traffic offenders are aliens — unfortunately the foreign driver who ran that red light was immediately identified as such; the fifteen Malaysians who committed the same crime looked like everybody else!

At the personal level, Malaysians see you as That Dane, or That Japanese or wherever you come from and will view your country by your behaviour.

"No, I would never let my children go to New Zealand. New Zealanders are irresponsible about children. I knew a New Zealander once who let his fourteen-year-old son drink beer!" Clear evidence that New Zealand is a nation of juvenile alcoholics...

All right, so it's none of their business. But expatriates in Malaysia come across all sorts of preconceived ideas about their countries and countrymen which had been planted here by predecessors. Think of that when you're being an unconventional free spirit!

Citizens of big countries are at a slight advantage here. For one thing, there are many Brits around (as compared to Danes, Nigerians or Italians), so Malaysians have a better sampling of what the British are like. Too fair an idea: I know English women who have to refuse gin-tonics, grimly, at each cocktail party they attend. Gin-tonic is what English women drink. Ask any bartender, any club boy, any Somerset Maugham novel or period film. How come you're English, and female, and prefer fresh fruit juice?

## STEREOTYPING

Malaysians who don't personally have much to do with foreigners still know quite a lot about them. This is thanks to the educational efforts of Hollywood — any regular viewer of Dallas and Dynasty can tell you as a "fact" that all Americans are rich, and all Americans are immoral. The normal American pregnancy is achieved by an octogenarian millionaire seducing/raping his adopted stepson's estranged common-law wife while she's in a three-week coma. Most likely in a speedboat shooting Niagara Falls, for the technical resources of the bigger film companies are truly awesome.

A correspondent to the local Press documented western immorality to his satisfaction by the fact that prostitution is legalized "in those parts". How much more moral to let VD spread naturally, unchecked by any official sanitary control! Reading the Letters to the Editor in a local paper is a good introduction to How the Malaysian Mind Works, as a matter of fact.

Stereotyping cuts both ways. Universal rules on Malaysian behaviour are stereotypes in their own way, too.

Take the well-known "facts" that:

"Malaysians are a calm, courteous people who abhor horseplay and hilarity." Few children on earth can be as beautifully behaved as Malay boys and girls who assist their parents' Hari Raya Open House celebrations — on the other hand, a wedding in Johor ends in a free-for-all water fight involving buckets and hoses from which all guests emerge dripping, dishevelled and screeching with laughter.

"Malaysians keep their voices down at all times", except when they don't and then they're quite as audible as any society professedly noisy.

"Malaysians never touch each other, this rule is observed even among family members if they are in public"; but watch this rule melt abruptly when people are struggling to board a bus or train!

"Malaysians always dress demurely", unless they're teenagers of all ages and like to wriggle their skinny shapes into miniskirts, tattered jeans, tank tops or whatever their respectable aunts disapprove of.

"Malaysians don't wear black, or off-white, except to funerals; these are the colours of mourning." Correct; but these may also be fashion colours. The younger Malaysians took up the mid-eighties fashion fad of swathing themselves in deep black quite as avidly as their Japanese friends did, and with the same reaction from the older generation. Many a family row centred on whether or not Miss could be allowed to visit her aged grandmother dressed in black jeans, a black T-shirt and a black jacket. And black sunglasses, and maybe she'd managed to get a black felt hat somewhere...

"Malaysians have a profound respect for the supernatural", but there are many sceptics who decline to be bound by outmoded superstitions. We have our rebels, iconoclasts, wild-eyed artists and razor-sharp thinkers who slash tradition and ceremony to tatters.

"Malaysians are naturally hospitable", true to a large extent, but politeness often prompts them to issue what is called a "chicken-style" invitation; if you turn up on their doorstep the next day you may actually be intruding!

If somebody you just met at a party invites you to "come to the house", thank them and ask what day or time would suit them, or for an exact address. "Oh any time...but we live in PJ and our house is a bit hard to find" is your cue to change the topic of conversation. "I usually have a few friends around for tea on a Tuesday afternoon" means she really wants you to come. If she offers exact directions on how to get to the house, scribbled on the back of a scrap of paper, she really wants you to come.

The notes I have put together give an outline of how Malaysians behave, and how they don't, when they're in a conservative mood. You have to know the rules before you can break them. In fact, the art of breaking rules consists in knowing them sufficiently well to know which one may be broken with impunity. Some people can do it, others diverge just a little bit and stand there looking pitiful, ill-mannered and uncouth.

## OF COUTH AND MANNERS

Couth and manners are intensely subjective concepts. Each culture has its own standards of acceptable table manners, for instance. In some countries a little food has to be left on the plate "for Miss Manners", in others a clean plate demonstrates the guest's appreciation of the meal. How may one person address another? Who may address whom? The manners of the highway have been codified into Traffic Regulations, but even in this wide-open field, much variety exists from country to country.

In Malaysia, public manners mostly concern touching and pointing. It is considered rude to touch another person, or to point at a person, animate creature or thing.

*Keeping your hands to yourself: Even in a crowded situation such as this, the "hands-off" stance is observed.*

## Touching

In a crowded street, it is of course impossible not to touch people. Manners demand that a walker in the crowd keep his hands near himself when he gets too near others, to demonstrate that he is not intending to touch anyone. If he is obviously going to push past people he lightly holds in his garments in a polite if ineffectual effort to prevent their brushing a passer-by. The others do the same; all parties involved know that they cannot help some slight touching, but making the effort counts for the deed and is appreciated. A person who strolls down a crowded street as if he was alone there, bumping and brushing against everyone, is considered very bad-mannered.

This applies particularly to contact between the sexes. A woman shopper does not cut into an oncoming group of men even if the market is very crowded. If she cannot avoid it, she holds her right arm stiffly down and presses an extended hand against her thigh, pushing her skirts or slacks towards herself.

Deliberate touching, as in handshaking, is acceptable in most introduction situations, indoors or out. Foreigners will usually find a Malaysian handshake a limp affair, more hand-touching than handshaking. Among conservative people, men don't shake hands with women; a respectful bow is substituted. (Among really conservative folks, women don't appear if male visitors are entertained, though they can be heard whooping it up in the kitchen.)

If a male foreigner is introduced to a Malaysian woman, he has to observe her behaviour carefully. If she gets ready to extend her hand, a shake is all right. If she clasps her own hands in front of her, it is safer to stick to bowing.

Grabbing a friend's arm, slapping his shoulder or patting his back if you're walking side by side is considered as "pawing" by many.

Malaysians who've been overseas, especially those who studied there for a few years, are fully aware that a European who lays an earnest hand on a friend's shoulder during a conversation is not making indecent overtures. But they, too, know that such excessive freedom is bad manners in Malaysia.

Aunts may pat or pinch a baby's cheeks to show affection (the idea is to make him laugh; he often has the sense to burst into loud howls on impact) but strangers should not touch anybody else's children. The European custom of patting children's heads and ruffling their hair is not appreciated in Southeast Asia; a person's head is a spiritually vulnerable part which unauthorized handling may injure!

## Kissing

Hand-kissing in a social context is out. There are some ceremonial occasions when family members kiss their elders' hands, but foreigners wouldn't be included in this ritual.

Social kissing, from "pecking" to the more elaborate modes, is much frowned upon in Malaysia though it is gaining ground among the yuppie set in towns. Standards vary widely; a hearty smack planted on a Malay *kampung* housewife's cheek might provoke a furious reaction not just from the injured husband but from the whole village!

The foreigner has to take his cue from the locals. If all the Malaysians present kiss each woman upon meeting, feel free to join in the fray; just don't get too thorough!

Babies and children are included in the no-kiss category. Close relatives may permit themselves such freedom, but even they practise restraint. Watch carefully! the fond granny isn't actually kissing but smelling and nuzzling the little faces.

## Hand Gestures

Pointing with one finger is very rude indeed, and only done as a deliberate insult.

Pointing at persons is worst of all. Pointing at animals is rude as well as risky; tradition has it that the beast's spirit will get its own back! Even pointing at the rainbow or moon is taboo. The way grannies tell it to their grandchildren, a rash index finger may drop off if it has been pointing at a heavenly body!

If there is a need to indicate somebody or something, do it with

the whole hand, or more discreetly with a thumb extended over a loosely doubled fist. An extended forefinger can be doubled back, so you actually "knuckle" the object you wish to point out. These are acceptable methods of pointing. A straight stabbing forefinger is NOT.

Other hand gestures, quite normal in some societies, are regarded as eccentric here. Only the comic character in a film slaps his forehead in despair, his thighs in delight, or hugs himself when he's happy. Pounding one fist into the palm of the other hand in exasperation is seen as a rude gesture by some Malaysians.

## Royalty, Protocol and You

At official functions, you even have to mind your feet! It is highly undecorous to sit with crossed legs if Royalty is present, or to let an unfortunate foot point at the guest of honour.

Should you be invited to attend a village function, maybe a wedding, where people sit on the floor, remember that men may sit cross-legged, women may not. Females sit with both feet tucked under to one side; after ten minutes they change sides to avoid serious circulation stoppages.

A person who is to be presented to Royalty must keep his or her hands loosely folded in the "at-ease" position except when actually bowing with both hands raised, palm-to-palm, to forehead level. But this is not a major issue here; people who are invited to official functions will be briefed on all the details of what they must, mustn't, may and may not do.

Any member of the public may come into contact with Royalty and other Big Shots in the street. The sound of sirens means you slow down and look in your mirror. Half a dozen traffic cops in formation bear down upon you and overtake; if one of them motions you to pull over to the left and stop, do so, letting whatever it is pass in style — the King, a Sultan, the Prime Minister, a Police chase, the Fire Brigade or an Ambulance. Any of these public calamities are heralded to the driving public by sirens in the street. Slow down first, then turn around to see what's going on. If the siren announces an official personage you're showing good manners. If it is only the police, you still risk bumping someone if you start gawking sideways and backward while your car is in motion.

There are nine Royal Houses in Malaysia. The reigning King is chosen from among them on a rotation basis. Pictures of the local Ruler and the King are found in most Government and many business offices.

Some foreigners are enchanted with the colourful ceremonies that accompany even a Royal Grandchild's First Walk — others of staunch egalitarian principle scoff at the expense and rigmarole involved.

You are allowed to think what you like, but outright criticism of this aspect of Malaysian life will be taken very, very badly. It is something like a family matter. Members may allow themselves the occasional muttered comment, but no outsider is invited to contribute his!

This applies not only to Royalty, but Malaysian life in general. Your comment, negatively, that "in my country we do things *this* way," must be very delicately worded to avoid giving offense. How many Americans could tolerate a Malaysian cook's exaltation of *gula melaka,* a healthy combination of natural sago and unrefined palm sugar, at the expense of sugar-laden overcooked fruit in a shell of artificially bleached flour and hydrogenated margarine, namely apple pie?

Does this mean that a foreigner in Malaysia is not allowed any views of his own unless they coincide with the Ministry of Tourism's publicity efforts? Not at all! Constructive criticism, sensitively expressed, is appreciated and taken note of. Ideally you should neither praise all Things Malaysian extravagantly, nor condemn them loudly, until you have been in the country a little while. Malaysians themselves are aware that some things are wrong here and there; they discuss them freely among themselves. They appreciate an outside viewpoint; they just don't like a grouch. Who does?

## FACE

Expats who have a lot do to with Malaysians at grassroot level often comment that these good folk are extremely touchy.

Malaysians themselves would say they have strong feelings of "shame", or they're concerned with keeping "face". "Face" and "shame" are the two sides of an emotional coin current throughout Southeast Asia. "Face" is a person's self-esteem; if it has been shattered by careless or deliberate assault, "face" is lost. Now the victim feels "shame" to the extent that he becomes sulky, uncooperative, in extreme cases even suicidal.

"Face" has a lot to do with what the neighbours think and vociferously, snickeringly say. A family, specifically the elders of the family, loses face if a son's or daughter's demeanour gives rise to comment. Disease is sometimes concealed because the daughters' chances of making good matches would be impaired. A mother or grandmother may have to pay for the family's "face" with her life — who'd want to marry into a family that is known to breed and propagate cancer? The unsuitable marriage of quite a remote relative can result in the break-off of family ties because "face" has been lost; as elsewhere on earth, the undeserving poor within the family fold are cast off much more readily than an eccentric, face-wasting but rich old uncle.

On the personal level, being directly scolded or made a fool of in public involves serious loss of "face". Expatriates should not reprimand their inferiors in front of other people, and be careful to choose impersonal expressions. There is a difference between: "The water tap has been left on and the washbasin overflowed!" and "You (silly girl!) left the water tap on and the washbasin overflowed!" The guilty party, your amah, will have to clean up the resulting mess anyway, so why rob her of "face" into the bargain? If there is a pecking order in the establishment, reprimands should come from the next higher level. The King didn't ask the dairy maid for butter personally, he sent the Queen to enquire. So it works in Malaysian society. If there are several servants in a household, the mistress informs the housekeeper that something has gone wrong, or should be done differently. The housekeeper will tick off the negligent party at the proper time and place and in the proper manner. This system works in a business context, too. Let the Chief Clerk keep the typists and tea ladies in order!

A person who made a promise and cannot keep it, a wrong prediction, loses "face" — more so if he is constantly and publicly reminded of the fact.

The Malay word *malu* is loosely translated as "shame". It can mean other things too. Young girls are expected to have "shame". If an aunt describes her niece as "shameful" she isn't implying what this would mean in English, but stating that the young lady is modestly bashful. A child who refuses to come and shake hands with visitors is excused on grounds of "shame". Young persons are generally expected to exhibit "shame" in front of their elders. They should keep quiet, move and act deferentially, not put themselves forward unnecessarily. Boys and girls acting shy towards each other are *malu* too, much to their elders' approval.

A middle-aged man says his piece confidently and competently, "but the first time I had to address a *kampung* meeting, I felt full of shame!" as he admits, and those present nod their heads. "We all felt shame when we were young," they agree, "it is only with increasing age that we get brave!"

This bravery is a social asset suitable to the middle-aged, not valour in the face of an enemy. The same aunt who commends her "shameful" niece may criticize the girl's friends as "too brave"; brave girls are noisy, cheeky, possibly inclined to flirt with the boys.

Young people starting on their first job may have to develop bravery beyond their years; the headmaster or inspector approves of a new trainee teacher who walks confidently into her first class as "not at all shameful; she's very brave!"

But the destructive shame, that which can in theory drive a person to suicide or the ungovernable frenzy called "amok", derives from loss of "face" perceived as personal insult. Laughing and jeering at a person, especially a newcomer or an outsider, will do it. Discussion of another's personal affairs, especially the skeletons in his cupboard, will shame him. Publicly administered reprimands, reprimands coming from the wrong source, give "shame". A domestic servant who is ticked off by smart-alecky children may leave her job rather than suffer the disgrace. Their mother may know nothing of the matter; the servant would certainly not complain to her!

Naturally tactful foreigners rarely encounter problems with "face"; they have their own feelings of self-esteem and know what would hurt, and what wouldn't. What they may not be aware of is the extreme force of public and societal opinion in this part of the world. What the neighbours say is of the utmost importance to a person who values his respectability, another word for "face". What the neighbours don't even say but blatantly think is even more important!

Only hermits are untroubled by "face" problems. The rest of us, if we lose it, feel "shame".

# Chapter Six

# WAYS OF SEEING
# — THEY AND YOU

Malaysia's population numbered about 18.6 million in 1992. Of this total, 59 per cent are Malays and other Bumiputera or "sons of the soil", 32 per cent are Chinese, and 8.2 per cent are Indians. All Malays and a number of Indians are Muslims.

## THE MALAY COMMUNITY

There is no shortage of posters and pamphlets depicting the typical Malay in his natural habitat: He dwells in an orange sunset under swaying coconut trees. He spends his time dancing in elegant silk pyjama suits, beating immense drums with long fretted spikes, beaching colourfully painted fishing boats on a strand of white sand, spinning hardwood tops, flying multicoloured kites in the deep blue sky or sitting on the doorstep of his leaf-thatched cottage looking hospitable. By way of earning a living, a pretty Malay girl, with much makeup and jewellery on, deposits a dainty ear of *padi* (rice) in a delicately worked little basket suspended from her gold brocade waist, smiling neither at her harvesting knife nor the *padi* stalks but straight into the camera.

## *Housing*

In real life, Malays look, act, work and worry about the same as everybody else. They may indeed live in leaf-thatched houses, they may also live in flats, in link houses, in semi-Ds, in mansions. Whatever the dwelling, it is likely to have an extended family in it. The uncle in town offers shelter to visiting relatives from the country, and "visiting" is liberally interpreted to include a nephew working in town for a few years.

When calling at a Malaysian house, it is customary to stop at the bottom of the steps and announce one's presence, or knock at the door and then wait. Nobody walks through an open front door uninvited; a man who does this is suspected of lecherous designs upon the women of the household!

After being invited in, the visitor takes off his shoes and leaves them at the door. He will be shown a place to sit; men usually assemble in the front verandah, women in an inner room. Friends of the housewife make informal calls at the kitchen door, but they wouldn't enter either until they have been asked.

A visitor is served a drink and offered snacks or cigarettes. Local people, especially the middle-aged, like to munch betel nut, a mild stimulant that is chewed with a leaf and lime paste. An expatriate may try it "for the experience", few like the pungent bite! It is obligatory to accept the drink and take at least a sip; to refuse food the rim of the dish must be touched with two fingers of the right hand. Food may never, never be handled or offered with the left hand!

## Names

Most Malay names are derived from the Arabic. A man may be called Ahmad bin Zain, Basri bin Abdullah, Rastam bin Khairul (Ahmad son of Zain, Basri son of Abdullah, Rastam son of Khairul). Typical women's names are Zaiton binte Ali, Fatimah binte Omar, Khadijah binte Salim (Zaiton daughter of Ali, Fatimah daughter of Omar, Khadijah daughter of Salim). This system of names also applies to Indian Muslims.

There are no surnames as the West knows them, and it is incorrect to address a man by his second name. Foreign teachers, used to calling their senior students "Smith" and "Jones" instead of Tom or Jack, have to beware of doing the same thing here. Ahiruddin bin Fauzi may be called "Din", but not Fauzi; Fauzi is his father! )

Malays keep track of their families right down to the remotest connection, though they don't usually call them by name; "eldest uncle, younger brother, youngest grandfather" are more likely forms of address within the family.

## Dress, Prayers

The majority of Malay men wear trousers and shirts, or suits if their offices are air-conditioned. Some wear a black velvet cap, the *songkok,* everyday; many wear it on Friday only.

Each Friday large numbers of Muslims attend congregational prayers at the mosque or *surau* ("chapel"). For this occasion they change into different clothes: the Arab-style robe may be worn, a loose jacket and long *sarung* (a kind of cotton tartan tuck-in kilt), or the Malay costume of a silk or cotton suit and a gold brocade *sarung* folded around the waist. Men must have their heads covered. Many wear the *songkok;* the haji who have performed the pilgrimage to Makkah wear a white skullcap or turban. In a hurry, it is enough to

*Every Malay neighbourhood has a mosque or village* surau.

drape a handkerchief over the head; boys who come to prayers straight from school sometimes do this.

In some States (Johor, Trengganu, Kelantan) Friday is the weekly holiday instead of Sunday. The business traveller must be aware of this. He will waste a trip if he is going north intending to negotiate a delicate deal in Kota Bharu on Friday!

In all States, Friday lunch hour starts at 11.30 a.m. and lasts till 2.30 p.m. to permit Muslims to attend prayers.

Malay women may choose between wearing western-style clothes, or the *baju kurung,* a full-length skirt with a long-sleeved overblouse that reaches to mid-thigh. Western-style may mean she is a modern miss who follows every fashion trend including mini-skirts, or she wears jeans and long-sleeved blouses and wraps her head in a silk scarf.

Traditionally, Malay women covered their hair with delicately embroidered muslin veils which were thrown over the head and loosely wrapped around neck and shoulders. A new fashion of tai-

*Malay schoolgirls in their white* baju kurung *and long* sarung.

lored coverings closely pinned over tight-fitting caps, strongly resembling the medieval goodwife's wimple and veil, is gaining ground among urban women of advanced views. One may occasionally glimpse a form presumably female swathed in black drapery from top to toe with just a sight slit, but this is not common.

Girls' school uniforms, compulsory in all government schools, give students the choice between a short-sleeved shirt blouse and pinafore dress, or a long *sarung* with a white *baju kurung*. Headdress is optional, but if worn it must be cap and veil pinned close under the chin.

It is left to the individual whether she wishes to wear a scarf or veil or not, except at prayers when head coverings are compulsory.

Muslims pray five times a day: Subuh at dawn, Zuhur at midday, Asar in the mid-afternoon, Maghrib at sunset, Isyak ("ishak") after dark. People may pray in their houses or at their workplace, mosques and *surau*. Many office buildings have a special "prayer room".

The exact time varies with the seasons and is regularly announced over the radio and TV. It is a good idea for foreigners to be aware of the prayer hours. Not all Muslims observe all five, but they must be given time to do so should they wish to. Visits and telephone calls should not be timed to coincide with prayer hours.

## *Ramadan*

During the month of Ramadan, Muslims fast from sunrise to sunset every day for 28 or 29 days. During this time, the usual welcoming drink of orange juice or tea is not offered, nor are cigarette boxes passed around. While it is legal for non-Muslims to indulge, it is very tactless to do so in front of their fasting friends!

Equally tactless is the question: "Are you fasting?" Not all Muslims fast, in fact not all of them have to: the eldery or infirm are exempt, as are pregnant or menstruating women and young children. But to ask an able-bodied man whether he is fasting implies the possibility that he might not be. Maybe he is, maybe he isn't, but you show much more respect if you assume he is, and refrain from serving or consuming anything in his presence.

Women among themselves have a little more freedom. A pregnant woman can be offered a drink; among friends one may mention that for the next three days she is not fasting. She wouldn't usually admit this in mixed company. A person who misses on a few days of the fast is expected to "make up" for the time lost later on.

The fasting month puts a lot of strain on Malay women. In a wealthy household with lots of servants, night is turned into day decorously; the sole-charge housewife on the other hand works at her job all day and then spends all night cooking.

Mama makes the crack-of-dusk breakfast. Served as soon as the sun sets, it is started with a sweetened iced drink followed by a big meal to make up for a lean day. After various snacks and tidbits the family goes to sleep. A meal has to be consumed before dawn, so mama is up at three a.m. to start the preparations. The steady toc-toc-toc of stone pestles grinding spices in mortars is heard in the wee hours of the morning throughout the land. After the early meal, the youngsters have to be got ready for school, some marketing done for the evening meal. If some of the children are too young to fast, mama has to cook for them in the daytime though she isn't allowed to taste or pick from the pot!

This explains why a usually keen tennis player may drop the sport for the duration. Provided she is not working, once husband and children have left and the house is clean she may be busy sewing new curtains, seat covers, clothes for the whole family. Towards the end of the month, she will also make cakes and biscuits for the great day of Hari Raya.

Traditional cakes can be bought, but many a woman prides herself on making the time-consuming delicacies for a special occasion at home. In the afternoon she will prefer catching forty winks to any sport at all, however healthy! Ramadan is not the time for social calling and dropping-in unless you have a pressing reason.

## Hari Raya

The right time to visit is at Hari Raya, the festival that concludes the fast and permits all participants to catch up on what they missed during the month. The New Moon has to be sighted on the last night of the month; anxious housewives keep the radio or TV on to listen for the official announcement from the Keeper of the Ruler's Seal. If the moon is sighted, Hari Raya follows the next morning. If not, another day of fasting has to be endured, and the day after that is Hari Raya by default. In some countries, the end of Ramadan is determined by calendar; Malaysia may decide to adopt this method.

In these days of ice boxes and corner shops, the urban housewife can usually manage to put off a major feast for one extra day. House-keepers in the rural areas, especially in areas where there is no power supply, have the chickens ready tied but still alive, the coconuts peeled but not yet grated while waiting for the announcement. A day's delay means a day's reprieve for the curry ingredients!

A few days before Hari Raya, some office workers invite all their

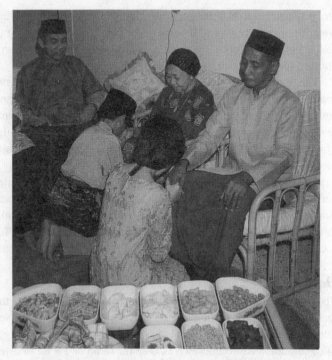

*Malay children kiss their parents' hands and beg for forgiveness on Hari Raya, the end of Ramadan.*

colleagues and friends to "come to the house"; others wish everybody Selamat Hari Raya and announce that they are going to *balik kampung,* to visit their parents' village for the occasion.

The last night of the fast pours seething masses of humanity into Malaysia's major traffic centres. The exodus may start a day or two earlier; the chances of sighting or not sighting the moon present a dilemma for people who only get the actual two days of Hari Raya off.

Bus, train and plane seats have been sold out weeks in advance, a point tourists and business travellers must be aware of. The night before Hari Raya turns all the roads out of Kuala Lumpur into bumper-to-bumper crawling lanes; the happy morn greets a quiet, empty city with shop shutters up and only a forlorn cop or two patrolling the void.

The picture in the suburbs is different. Families go out in the morning to visit grandparents, kiss their elders' hands and beg forgiveness for any sins committed during the past year. Mosques overflow for Hari Raya Prayers. Everybody is wearing new, festive clothes, houses are decorated with lights which twinkle through the night, with bunting and strips of tinsel which flap in the breeze as visitors stream in through the wide open doors.

Hari Raya is a wonderful excuse for visiting, even people one doesn't know very well. New arrivals in the country should persuade a friend to take them visiting. Every household welcomes friends' friends even unto the third remove; the student of curry will find Hari Raya the best possible opportunity for some serious research.

Hari Raya visitors are welcomed at the door and invited in. They should remove their shoes; in modern households they are sometimes encouraged to leave them on. They shake hands with their host and hostess, wishing them "Selamat Hari Raya" (peaceful Hari Raya), then make the round of the assembled guests with the same blessing.

Visitors are directed where to sit, and offered drinks and a succession of tidbits from trays. After a little small talk, the hostess or her daughters urge guests to come and taste a little bit of "our poor, common curry." A huge spread is set out, curries, relishes, chutneys, mounds of white rice and yellow rice and almond rice and raisin rice...

The true art of Hari Raya visiting is to taste a little of everything but not too much. The appetite has to be severely rationed for all the other houses still to be visited. Families keep count of who came and who didn't; especially in the *kampung* it is almost impossible to visit houses three, five and seven but omit one, two, four and six! And how would you explain to two of seven friends that you visited the other five, but not them...?

Hari Raya is celebrated by Muslims of all races and all stations. Indian Muslims have their own varieties of curries and sweetmeats unheard-of by their Malay brethren; some Pakistani lamb ragouts are stewed in almond cream instead of the coconut milk. The Prime Minister keeps Open House at certain hours; this may be an expatriate's only chance to set foot inside Sri Perdana (the official residence) and see the great man close up!

Most foreign guests will be impressed by the manners of Malay children during a festival. Dressed in miniature versions of adult costume, they help their parents receive visitors, gravely shake hands with all comers, hand around trays if they are old enough. The boys may eventually get tired of too much good behaviour and sneak off to play with the new toys they got for Hari Raya, or to burn fire crackers and fire bamboo cannons. Small children are looked after by bigger sisters or granny, handed from aunt to aunt, rocked in a cloth cradle if they feel sleepy or fretful.

Malays are very fond of children, and consider them one of heaven's greatest gifts. Many Malay families adopt infants in addition to their own, often girls — they harbour no prejudice against female children. If the *kampung* system of child-rearing is short on discipline, it is very long on affection. A small child is petted and indulged by all; elderly people count grandchildren as the richest blessing of old age.

## Pregnancy and Childbirth

As soon as it is known that a young woman is pregnant, she is subject to certain taboos to safeguard her own and her baby's health. These vary from region to region and with the educational status of the mother and her family. Some expectant mothers are prepared to pay token observance to custom while they are visiting their parents' house, but live "the modern life" as career women in town. Others like to be lulled in the security of traditions and taboos, safely hedged around by mama and a team of anxiously clucking aunts.

Traditionally, a pregnant woman may not kill, tie or mangle anything. Disregard of these taboos may result in birth marks, or a deformed baby. Fire or water may not be carried behind her back. She is not allowed to look at anything ugly or frightening — a rather subjective prohibition which forbids monkeys, some other animals and dead bodies but allows unrestricted consumption of TV blood-and-gore.

A pregnant woman's husband is not allowed to kill or tie animals either, to nail or lash timber, to block holes or dam little rivers. He is obliged to procure any foodstuffs she may have a fancy for.

A horde of evil spirits inhabits the jungle, air and water of Malaysia, invisibly lurking. Many of them specialize in pregnant women. A married man is advised to plant a pineapple under his house to hamper one particularly unpleasant ghoul that drifts around at dusk with its guts trailing along behind, eagerly slobbering for a woman with child. The spikes of the pineapple leaf will catch this revolting spectre so it cannot make its way up the steps. I have not been able to obtain practical directions on how to dispose of a baby-eating harpy caught by its own entrails on a pineapple plant under one's house, however.

When the woman's pregnancy reaches the seventh month, her mother officially engages the midwife who will conduct the "bathing the womb" ceremony. The expectant mother's hair is trimmed, she is massaged with fragrant oils and given a bath in scented water. Various rites are performed to divine the baby's sex. From now on, the midwife is in charge. If necessary she will call in a *bomoh* (traditional healer) for a bit of preventive medicine to supplement the pineapple plant.

Childbirth is strictly a women's affair. The midwife rules supreme, aided and abetted by mother, mother-in-law or other married women. Many West Malaysian villages have a hospital-trained nurse-midwife, often in charge of the general clinic plus two or three maternity beds. In towns, babies are usually born in hospital, though district midwives are on call for people who prefer home deliveries.

The occasional exasperated appeal by a medical officer to halt dangerous obstetric practices like applying external pressure to a labouring woman's abdomen shows that some bad old customs are still observed. There are very few places in West Malaysia where a maternity patient does not have access to trained medical staff; those who put themselves into the hands of the local Wise Woman do so of their own choice.

After the baby has been born, the cord is cut with a sharp bamboo sliver. The afterbirth is handed to the father to bury in a carefully selected spot. This may be a device for keeping him out of the way; he certainly wasn't at his wife's bedside during labour! But after baby has been washed and swaddled, it is handed to the father or in his absence the grandfather who now whispers the Call to Prayer into the tiny ear.

There is deep significance in this ritual. The Call to Prayer are the first spoken words a Muslim hears; they will be the last addressed to his lifeless form prior to burial. Malays value an eloquent speaker, but Hearing the Word comes first!

Mother and baby are anointed with a variety of medicines designed to warm them and keep the "wind" away from them. Immediately after delivery, the baby had betel nut juice applied all over his body. Now he is rubbed with a lotion containing turmeric, ginger and other spices. He lies beside his mother on her bed, behind closed mosquito curtains; it is only on the seventh day that he is transferred into a cloth cradle suspended from the ceiling of the room.

On the baby's seventh day, a small ceremony is held in the

parents' house. The little one should receive a name on this occasion, though in these days of national registration many happy fathers have pre-empted custom.

If the baby already has a birth certificate, the name is confirmed on the seventh day. The men of the family carry the infant into the front room of the house, where the eldest and most respected carefully cuts off a few strands of his hair. Rice paste and rose water are dabbed on the child's forehead and he is officially "given" his name. The women repeat the hair-cutting in the inner room, then the baby is returned to his mother and laid in his cloth cradle.

The floor around the bed is scrubbed to cleanse it of any blood that may have stained it. The midwife is given her fee and traditional tokens.

Then the baby's tongue is "sweetened": tiny quantities of betel nut juice, honey and salt are applied to it with a gold ring. This is to make the child "speak eloquently and with wit before princes, so that his voice may be sweet like honey to delight men's hearts, that his words may be as savoury as betel nut and their purport as effective as salt."

A tall order for a tiny bundle of humanity just seven days old, but remember: he heard the Word first!

The mother's period of confinement, if the resident granny is a person of strong character, lasts from 28 to 44 days.

All Malaysian communities observe some confinement restrictions. It is a moot point whether the Malays learnt from the Chinese, the Indians from the Malays or the Chinese from the Indians that a new mother must be kept indoors and hampered hand and foot. She is not allowed to leave the house on any pretext, she must not open doors and windows because "wind" would be bad for her and her baby. Neither mother nor child can go for a ride in a car, not with all the windows shut, not for any reason.

The mother can't eat any "cold" foods, and cold has nothing to do with intrinsic temperatures. There are such things as "cooling" infusions and gruels, eaten by people who are overheated. But a newly delivered mother is by definition cold; "cold" foods would aggravate her condition! Most vegetables, however freshly cooked and steaming hot, are "cold" and therefore off the menu. So are fruit and iced drinks. A bath or shower would do the new mother untold harm. She is grudgingly allowed to swab herself with a damp towel if she feels sticky. Shampooing the hair is another no-no, and all this lasts for 44 days.

Not many women, rural or urban, put up with the full rigours of this regimen. Much depends on personalities and on circumstances. A working woman (whether she be a company director or a farmer) may observe custom for a week or two, and then sneak back to work. In a household full of willing and competent helpers, the mother can choose to take six weeks off if she likes.

Working women in professional and clerical jobs usually get two full months of maternity leave; it is up to them and their attendants how many days of this period she wants to spend "in confinement". Their daily-paid sisters resume work as soon as possible to supplement the household finances; confinement pampering increases in intensity in direct porportion to the family's means!

The sole-charge urban housewife, even if she has a household helper or a temporary "confinement amah", knows that the longer she stays out of circulation the worse a state the house will be in when she finally emerges from her seclusion. I know one Malay woman who used to do a bit of housework on the quiet but quickly leapt back into bed if she heard visitors approaching. They expect to find her languidly drooping among pillows, sipping tepid water with ginger juice by way of a warming cocktail. "They would have reported me to my mother-in-law if they'd seen me mopping the kitchen floor!"

Friends visit the new mother during her confinement, bringing gifts and congratulations. In town it is usual to announce such visits by telephone to find out what is a convenient time.

The forty-fourth day marks the mother's return to normal. It is celebrated with a small party, within the family or with some invited guests who partake of a festive meal and bring presents of money, baby clothing or tokens of gold. This is also the occasion when baby first treads the ground.

Of course he is far too small to attempt anything like walking. There are various ways of treading the earth: grandmother may hold a handful of earth against his pink soles, he may be held "standing up" while his feet touch the ground briefly. In some farming areas, a winnowing tray containing earth and seven of its fruit (sweet potato, cassava, corn cobs, bananas, yams, etc) is brought into the house, and baby is held to "stand" among these. If his head hasn't been shaved yet, this ceremony can also be performed on the forty-fourth day.

## Childhood and Rites of Passage

At the age of starting primary school, Malay children are enrolled with a Koran tutor. The Koran teacher may be an elderly man known for his learning and piety. In some areas a woman teaches the scriptures, especially to girls.

In a Malay household, the Koran itself is treated with great respect. Every reader washes his or her hands before handling the book. Many people keep it in a case or a cloth covering. No other books may be laid on top of the sacred volume, which is usually put on a special stand for reading so it will not be defiled by dust from the floor.

When they first start their lessons, the children are dressed in their holiday costumes and brought to the Koran teacher by their parents. A number of gifts accompany the enrolment, prominent among them a stout little cane which the teacher is supposed to use as an inducement to learning.

The Koran is written in Arabic; the new student has to master the script first of all. Then comes the reading of words, then sentences. In the old days, few Koran students understood the language they were reading; it was enough to be able to read and pronounce the words.

When a boy has completed reading through the Holy Book once, his basic studies are considered at an end. A family party is given in the scholar's honour, usually a small feast to which close relatives and the teacher are invited. The boy, dressed in his holiday best, thanks his teacher and begs forgiveness for any pranks and nonsense that may have enlivened the study period. Then he is asked to read selected passages from the Book to demonstrate his knowledge.

Sometimes several families celebrate their children's accomplishment together, especially if they are related. A cousin's wedding may also serve as the occasion. The house is already full of kith and kin so the boy will have a good audience; they in turn appreciate a suitable diversion while awaiting the arrival of the groom and the beginning of the festivities.

Children are usually given presents of clothing, books or toys after they have completed reading the Koran.

Most Malay girls have their ears pierced when they are still quite young. It is a simple operation, usually performed by one of the female relatives. A needle with several strands of cotton is used to pierce the earlobe, the thread is left hanging to drain the small wound and prevent the hole from closing. When the perforation is considered healed, a gold stud or small earring is inserted.

Some families have their little girls' ears pierced by the family doctor nowadays. Jewellers will perform the task free if a pair of ear studs are bought at the same time.

Malay boys are circumcised before their teens, usually after they have completed reading the Koran. This minor operation is often carried out by a doctor in the privacy of his surgery, and the attendant festivities kept to a minimum. In a conservative society, however, it is a public spectacle much enjoyed by everyone except those directly concerned.

On the morning of the day, all the boys to be circumcised are taken for a prolonged bath in the river by one of the elders. Immersion in cold water is supposed to soften and numb the skin.

When the time is judged right, the lads are brought back to the village. Here, "Tok Mudim", the circumciser, has set up his equipment in a curtained-off area in a house. Each boy in turn sits astride a freshly felled banana trunk, and the expert performs his job with a few swift strokes of a sharp knife.

The boys' families and half the village are assembled in the same house, but of course they aren't allowed to watch. They don't particularly want to listen, either; prayers and blessings are chanted, audibly, until the last boy has been "done" and Tok Mudim puts his instruments away. A dressing of traditional medicine is applied, then the boy is made to rest under a man's *sarung* suspended from the centre to remove pressure from the sore spot.

A festive meal is served to all present. Tok Mudim gets his fees and traditional tokens, he leaves a supply of dressings with the patient's parents. Boys are under a number of taboos until they are fully healed: they may not take two helpings of food, they may not cut anything with shoots or spikes, they may not drink coconut water, they may not run around. On the first couple of days, very few want to run around anyway.

In some communities, the newly circumcised boys are attended to by men, and only served food cooked for them by a man. They have to put up with a little good-natured masculine teasing now they have entered the world of grown-ups; little brothers regard them with awe and fear born of the knowledge that it will be their turn next.

## Marriage

In the old days, every Malay marriage was arranged. Young people were not supposed ever to meet those of the other sex; the avid student of Malay literature wonders where the classical authors got the material for their many beautiful and often tragic love stories from!

In real life, young people don't mix without restraint, but they do know each other. A shy fellow may ask his mother to make the first moves, but he wouldn't direct her to a girl whom he dislikes, a girl who dislikes him, or a girl whom he knows to be totally unacceptable to the family.

Even if the young couple have found and chosen each other, many families still go through the traditional motions of "finding a bride" for their son.

A delegation of aunties and uncles is sent to the young woman's house. They are welcomed and asked to take a seat. After some discussions on the crops and the weather, one of the daughters serves drinks.

Ah, that must be Minah! haven't seen her since she was a little girl. Faridah is married, isn't she? and dear Minah must be engaged? Not yet? Well, well...of course, who can blame a mother for keeping the treasure of her heart at home for a few more years! It seems to be quite the thing nowadays for young people to marry later. Take our cousin Faizal — his son Amin isn't married yet, though he is working at a very good job. University graduate, you know. A good boy, is Amin. Though he lives in town he doesn't go chasing good-for-nothing girls the way some of these young fellows do. Oh, we don't know what plans his parents have for him, but if they heard of a really nice girl...

This is the cue for the young woman's aunts to put in a good word. Minah disappeared into the kitchen after she has served the drinks and demurely greeted everybody, so they are free to speak. Industrious, pious, frugal, virtuous, deferential to her elders; it wouldn't do for us to praise our own niece, but where can you find such a good girl in this wicked modern world? If some of the family have literary talents, a few *pantun* (quatrains) embellish the occasion; much fun is had by all.

Nobody talks bluntly of matching Amin with Minah, that would be uncouth. "Flowers blossoming unseen by any but the discerning" may be mentioned, "the joys of kindred hearts and souls meeting" are in order, "the blessings of a united thriving family" may be praised in principle. The advance party returns to the boy's family with a good report, but so far nobody is committed in any way.

"The funny thing", says a University lecturer who recently got engaged, "is that Zul and I meet in the staffroom every day. We only informed our parents after he had proposed to me! But his granny insisted that everything be done "properly", so we are going through the whole traditional rigmarole. It's sort of sweet, I guess, but we could have got married all by ourselves if we'd wanted to!"

The whole traditional rigmarole entails another visit to the young man's house, this time by his mother. She has a serious discussion with the girl's mother; if the outcome is satisfactory she places a gold ring on her future daughter-in-law's finger. The lucky man is neither present nor needed. Engagements and wedding preparations are women's business.

One important part of the discussion is about expenses. Who pays for what? how many feasts will there be, in whose house?

For a grand traditional wedding, the couples' outfits are made of a length of silk brocade richly shot with gold thread, specially ordered for the occasion. This thumping item of expense is paid for by the man's family; even on a more modest scale, he has to provide his bride with wedding clothes, perfumes and toiletries.

Gifts are often brought from the groom's to the bride's house in a gaily costumed procession of young girls. Trays laden with food are carried shoulder-high, displays of flowers contain banknotes folded into blooms, birds, fans and other fancy shapes. A bunch of little boys noisily beating tambourines precedes the gift-bearers; let the whole *kampung* know and appreciate how lavishly Amin is treating his bride-to-be and his future in-laws!

Specific wedding customs vary from area to area, from family to family. Many households have a women's party on the night before the wedding. The bride invites her maiden companions for a Koran-reading session which is concluded with an all-female supper. In rural *kampung,* where many wedding guests come from far away and stay for a few days, this is more common than in town. An elderly woman attendant called Mak Andam trims the bride's hair and applies henna to her hands and feet after the reading.

The two essentials to legalize the marriage are the groom's declaration and the *bersanding.*

The groom has to declare his intention of marrying the young woman to her father, in the presence of witnesses and mosque officials. These elders may be in a frolicsome mood and insist that he repeat the formula, louder. Repeat it again, in one breath — and so on, until they are satisfied that he meant what he said. The documents are then signed, and the young couple is officially married, though not yet living together. The *bersanding,* held on the same day or the next, will publicly ratify the union.

Wedding guests have been converging on the bride's house since morning. They bring presents which are handed to a member of the family, discreetly or openly as local custom dictates. In some areas, an elderly uncle sits near a brass tray; each time a gift of money is received he drops an antique coin into the tray with a resounding "ping" so the assembled company may note the guest's generosity. In most cases, donations are recorded by the family and later acknowledged. Within a close-knit rural community, the celebrating family "owes" all donors for gifts in cash, kind or kitchen-duty time; such debts fall due when another family hosts a celebration of some sort.

The *bersanding* is a sitting-in-state, theoretically the first time the young couple meet. The bride is seated on one of two chairs on an elevated platform, or on a richly decorated bed. The noise of the

*Gorgeously attired Malay bride and groom sit side by side at a* bersanding *which publicly ratifies the union.*

bridegroom's procession is heard outside, but she may still have a little while to wait.

Although the groom is carried, paddled or driven from his house to hers in splendour, with drums beating and flags flying, he may not be allowed in. Members of the bride's household vociferously refuse him entry. They've no idea who he is or what he wants! A bribe ostentatiously administered by the Best Man jogs their memories, and they open the door.

In some areas, an armed man denies entry to the bridegroom's party. The Best Man whips out his kris too, and a mock-fight ensues up and down the steep wooden staircase, encouraged and commented upon by the women leaning out of all the windows — but of course the Best Man wins. He escorts his friend into the bride's presence, seats him beside her, and takes up his place as guard of honour behind the chair, out of breath but triumphant. Being Best Man in a Malay village is no sinecure!

Now the married couple sit side by side, forbidden to look at each other after a couple of stolen glances while the groom is

103

helped to his seat. Gorgeously dressed men, maidens and "slave children" surround and guard them, as do a few elderly women including Mak Andam who is officially in charge. A tray equipped with flasks and fancy bowls stands near. The couple sit with their hands on their knees, eyes cast down, while the assembled company can admire the beauty and comeliness of the spectacle and some prayers are said. Then the elders get up, in order of seniority, to bless the bride and groom.

Each person dabs a touch of sandalwood paste on the groom's forehead, sprinkles him with rose water from one of the flasks, applies the same to the backs of his hands, and finally tosses a few grains of rice and a few flower petals over his head. Regional customs vary; maybe a gold ring suspended from a stingray tail is also touched to the young man's forehead, the sandalwood is supplemented with rice flour paste. The same procedure is repeated with the bride. Then the next well-wisher comes forward, then the next. Uncles feel free to make all sorts of ribald comments during the *bersanding;* woe betide the bride or groom who laughs or even smiles!

No wedding is complete without a feast. Bands of willing helpers have been toiling in the kitchen since dawn, but before the assembled company can tuck in the young couple have got to eat the "rice of first meeting". Sweet glutinous is served to them. He has to feed her, she has to feed him. Now at last they're allowed to look at each other, "but they're gazing into each other's eyes instead of attending to the matter in hand!" a witty cousin hollers. The first few morsels of rice usually miss their destination, but Mak Andam lends a hand and finally everyone can start enjoying the feast.

Upon departure, each guest is given a decorated hard-boiled egg, symbol of fertility. Foreign guests should be warned: there is no provision for Kissing the Bride at a Malay wedding!

In town, where most weddings are provisioned by professional caterers, the *bersanding* platform, bed and room decorations, even the bride's and groom's outfits may be rented. The caterers also provide the eggs daintily packaged in little baskets or tinsel frills. In a village, part of the fun is for the guests to see what sort of finery and drapery the happy family can provide. The bride's sisters and aunts often spend hours, days, cutting and stitching, plaiting miniature baskets for the hundreds of eggs that will be presented to the guests.

Next morning, the newly married couple are dragged out of bed at the crack of dawn. Dressed in their night clothes, they are made to sit on the kitchen steps where they are given a thorough bath with buckets of water poured over their heads. In the southern States, this degenerates into a free-for-all water fight, concluding with a hilarious early breakfast after all the belligerents have huddled on some dry clothing. From first to last, the women of a *kampung* household put a lot of work into organizing and provisioning a wedding, but they get a lot of fun out of it too!

## *Funeral*

As soon as a Malay has died, a member of the family hurries to inform the mosque officials of the death. As many relatives as possible are summoned; telephone and telegraph supplement the old-time messenger. Anybody who has been notified of a death in the family must attend at once if he possibly can; this applies even to fairly distant kin.

The body is laid on a mat or low bed until it can be washed and shrouded. A cloth is suspended over it to protect it from dust that might fall from the ceiling; a pair of betel nut clippers is laid on its waist to keep ghouls away.

After washing and shrouding, the body is laid on a mat and covered with cloth. A fine veil is put over the face to permit the mourners, now pouring in thick and fast, to take one last glance at the departed. Incense is burnt in a censer on the floor, prayers are said. Mourners turn up on the doorstep, dressed in sombre colours, carefully avoiding unnecessary noise or frivolous chatter. Most bring a small present of money. Neighbours' wives help in the kitchen as the bereaved family has to offer food and drink to all comers.

The burial usually takes place within twenty-four hours of the death. If a person died during the night, he may be buried the following afternoon; the climate does not permit a lengthy period of lying-in-state.

In some regions, the body is laid on a bier and covered with a pall. More common is a bottomless coffin, the body resting on a taut cloth nailed around the lower base.

The bier or coffin is carried shoulder-high by male relatives, protected by one or more umbrellas. It is sometimes taken to the local mosque or *surau* where it is laid in the niche facing Makkah. Here prayers are said while younger family members or neighbours are digging the grave. These prayers may also be read in the house, and the body taken straight to the graveyard after their completion.

The coffin, if one is used, is lowered into the grave; otherwise the corpse is taken off the bier and laid straight in the earth. Two family members stand in the grave to position the body correctly, and put clods of earth next to it in the coffin. Then the Call to Prayer is recited over the departed for the last time. The helpers climb back to the light of day and the grave-diggers complete their task.

After the grave has been closed, senior mosque officials protected by a ceremonial umbrella recite some prayers. They sprinkle the newly dug earth with sandalwood water and flower petals. Wooden markers are commonly used in Malaysia, sometimes replaced by tombstones after the earth on the new grave has settled.

The bereaved family will invite close relatives for a meal in memory of the deceased on the third, seventh, fourteenth, fortieth and hundredth day after his death. The Hundredth Day is often the occasion for placing the tombstone, if one is used, and an offcial end to mourning. Some families hold a memorial feast on the anniversary of the death.

*Chinese lanterns decorate a street during Chinese New Year.*

## THE CHINESE COMMUNITY

The bulk of Malaysia's Chinese population is descended from fairly recent immigrants; others have been here for hundreds of years.

Malaysian market towns strongly resemble townships in southern China, the origin of most Malaysian Chinese. These shophouses are in fact link houses ranged along a covered verandah, the "five-foot way" as the sidewalk is called. The business premises are downstairs, the family lives upstairs or at the back.

"Shophouse Chinese" men are sometimes seen wearing long baggy shorts and singlets, the latter rolled up to expose comfortably rounded bellies. Rubber sandals, locally known as "slippers", complete his get-up — but let nobody be fooled by appearances! The balding rather shabbily dressed gentleman who is supervising the weighing of rubber sheets on the pavement in front of his shophouse may have a considerably bigger bank balance than the

107

owner of the Mercedes that's parked a few doors away outside a Finance Company.

Some older women wear black silk trousers and blue or floral blouses. The floral cotton "samfoo" trouser suit is already getting old-fashioned but shopkeepers, stall-keepers, snack-sellers often wear them.

It is around the farms, small towns and in the New Villages that the *oto* may be seen, that peculiar bottomless patchwork apron that covers a toddler's chest and belly but leaves the rest of him bare. Its purpose is to prevent "wind" from getting into his little body through the belly-button! For some reason toddlers wearing *oto* look much more naked than *kampung* urchins with never a stitch on.

Most Malaysian Chinese wear western clothes, from casual to fashionable to impeccably elegant, as their work, tastes and means dictate. Even for holidays and festivities, very few of them dress up in the traditional robes of their ancestors, though women with legs worth displaying may wear the skin-tight, high-slit *cheong-sam*.

The black fashion wave in the mid-80s had its adherents in Malaysia too, despite the well-known fact that "Chinese never wear black except to funerals." Some youngsters even turned up in deep black at New Year Celebrations, a deplorable state of affairs commented upon in the Letters column of more than one local newspaper.

Some elderly Chinese ladies, especially if they are widows, wear black silk clothes for weddings and other solemnities. To make the point that the event is festive, gold and jade jewellery is also worn.

The gorgeous costumes of the baba and nonya, "Straits Chinese" who have lived in Malacca since the 15th century, are only worn for formal purposes or at cultural shows nowadays. Very, very few Straits Chinese couples get married in the old-fashioned garments, with the old-fashioned pomp that was considered necessary for a proper wedding in their grandparents' day.

## *Names*

Chinese names consist of three parts: the family name, the generation name and the personal name. Mr Tan is called Tan Cho Meng; friends call him Cho Meng or Ah Meng. It is not correct to call him Mr Meng!

His wife's name is Sim Siaw Lian; at work she may be addressed as Mrs Tan, or Madam Sim, but her friends call her Siaw Lian or Ah Lian. Repeating the Ah adds a little softness to yelling for somebody: Ah Meng ah! Ah Lian ah!

Relatives don't call each other by name, they use kinship terms: younger uncle, second aunt, youngest sister-in-law, elder great-uncle. A newly married-in family member has to learn all these things as soon as possible to avoid saying the Wrong Thing!

One of the purposes of the tea ceremony that used to solemnize a Chinese wedding was that the young couple should formally meet, and learn to recognize, their new relations. Tea was served to the elders in strict order of seniority; a bride or groom with an excellent-memory might remember all the names and status titles after the event.

English-educated or Christian Chinese often give a Christian name to their children; some adopt one without the religious connotations. Mr Tan is Joseph Tan Cho Meng, his wife is Agatha Sim Siaw Lian. Such names may or may not appear on birth certificates or identity cards, but they are commonly used for all but official purposes.

A few Chinese names consist of only two parts: Chin Peng, Pang Ling; a very few run to four. In any case, the first is his surname.

The spelling and pronunciation of the same Chinese name vary from dialect to dialect. Mr Wong is also Hwang or Wee, Mr Goh, Ngu or Wu. A Chinese scholar differentiates between the many ideograms that are used to write names. He determines whether Goh and Wu are related, and reveals that one Ong is not connected in any way with another Ong— they don't use the same root character.

Not all Chinese could figure out these distinctions for themselves. There is quite a large English-educated (or, nowadays, English-and-Malay-educated) group among them; while most can sign their own names in ideograms they would be in no position to draw philological deductions, or even read the Chinese newspaper!

## *Religion*

Under "religion", most non-Christian Chinese will put "Buddhist" on a census form. This term covers all shades of opinion, from the strictly vegetarian philosopher, monk or nun to the idol-worshipper to the complete agnostic who only burns a few joss sticks from time to time to please his aged mother. The great majority of Chinese consider their parents' feelings as much more important than the gods'!

The Chinese temples generally seen in Malaysia cater for a "folk version" of Buddhism or Taoism, peopled by a multitude of gods and goddesses each in charge of one particular aspect of human activity. Special problems or requests may be brought before the deities by presenting them with joss sticks, flowers or fruit. A wealthy person may bequeath some of his or her estate for the upkeep of an old temple or the endowment of a new one; such generosity ensures the donor of blessings in the after-life and perpetuates his descendants' prosperity.

Many temples have facilities for fortune-telling. There may be a resident medium who predicts the future in a variety of ways. The supplicant is given a quiver full of long bamboo sticks, he shakes the vessel till one or several fall out, then the medium interprets the cryptic messages inscribed on each. Some mediums go into a trance and prophesy in that condition.

There are temple festivals on occasions such as the resident god's birthday, the full moon on the fifteenth of each month, or local holidays. Vesak Day, the birthday of the Buddha, is celebrated with prayers in temples and Buddhist monasteries; the lay popula-

*A devotee at a Chinese temple burns incense to give thanks and to ask for blessings.*

tion organizes colourful processions.

During the Seventh Month, the spirits of the dead are abroad and need to be fed and entertained with lavish operatic performances to which the living are, fortunately, also invited. The Autumn Moon Festival in the eighth month is celebrated with a special kind of very rich pastry, the Moon Cake, paper lanterns and family dinners. This is the time of weddings, for the huge autumn moon is considered a

111

good omen for prosperity.

Christian Chinese do not usually participate in these occasions, though anybody of whatever denomination is free to eat moon cakes, dragon festival dumplings and other seasonal delicacies.

## *Chinese New Year*

The Chinese New Year, however, is not properly considered a religious festival. It is a day of family reunions, a day to pay one's respects to the elders, a day of feasting and fun and gambling; in the old days it was often the only holiday the working classes took all year. Malaysians of other races visit their Chinese friends on Chinese New Year, business grinds to a standstill for a few days and fire crackers (some types are officially tolerated if not encouraged) shatter the eardrums.

Chinese families have been busy preparing cakes and tidbits, scrubbing the house from top to bottom and making new clothes for all members. It is almost impossible to get a new dress made a few weeks before Chinese New Year — the dressmakers have been booked out months ahead!

As the day draws near, some people quietly "escape" for a few days. They put an advertisement in the local paper, to the effect that "Mr and Mrs Tan wish their friends and relatives a Happy Chinese New Year, and desire to inform them that they will not be celebrating the festival in Kuala Lumpur." Maybe they visit their parents in their hometown, maybe they're sneaking off to Lake Toba for a week.

There is an elaborate family dinner on New Year's Eve, accompanied by many toasts. The New Year Day itself is so auspicious that the house may not be swept on the first day — all the good luck would be swept out too, and who can risk that?

While happy revellers are anxious to test their individiual good luck by gambling, pious children bow to their elders and are given *ang pow* ("red packets") in return. These oblong red paper envelopes contain gifts of money; the children of visitors, especially on the first day of the new year, will also be given red packets. Flowers and red oranges are heaped on the family altar, joss sticks and candles are lit; Christian churches have special New Year prayers for their Chinese congregation.

Visitors start to turn up at their Chinese friends' houses at about 10 a.m., an uninterrupted stream that won't end till after dark. They are entertained to the best there is, and this includes rivers of fine liquor though soft drinks are kept in reserve for those who prefer them. Trays of cakes and snacks are handed round, newcomers shake hands while an earlier batch of visitors is leaving.

Small talk has to be kept carefully within auspicious bounds. Things like "illness, failure, death, bad luck, bankruptcy" may not be mentioned. In this modern world, "politics" is also blacklisted, and for the same reason: talking of trouble amounts to inviting it!

Convivial parties gather to eat raw fish at Chinese New Year time. This dish is considered highly auspicious because its Chinese name, *yu sheng*, may also be interpreted to mean "over-abundance". A KL doctor who can't speak for the intangible qualities of the dish says he gets a number of food poisoning cases each Chinese New Year. "If you must eat raw fish," he warns, "see to it that it is fresh fish, freshly prepared. Some restaurants cut and marinate the fish and leave it lying around in the kitchen for up to two days, to have it in readiness each time a customer orders it!"

No such danger attends the consumption of vegetarian meals, *fatt choi* which may be interpreted to mean "Buddha's Vegetables" and is sure to shower prosperity upon the pious diners.

Chinese New Year officially ends at *chap ngo mei*, the fifteenth day of the lunar year. Many families have one more reunion dinner, cosier but not as grand as the New Year one. In the old days, *chap ngo mei* was the day on which unmarried urban maidens were allowed out of the house (for once), and taken to the waterfront in rickshaws or cars. They threw oranges into the sea or river while praying for good husbands. In many cases these must have been self-fulfilling prayers. The young men of the town, dressed up to the nines, just happened to be strolling along that same waterfront, determined to get a nod or a wink right under the nose of their best girls' chaperones.

Another *chap ngo mei* custom is fire-walking, celebrated at some temples. A number of mediums, usually male, work themselves into a trance. When the master of ceremonies judges the time right, he makes them trot down a 3-metre long pit of burning charcoal. As a bit of light relief they also jog the same distance on broken glass, or climb up a ladder made of swords. Such an exercise is often undertaken to redeem a vow, or to support a supplication. After the fire-walk, the devotee wakes up with the soles of his feet unharmed.

## Pregnancy and Childbirth

All Malaysian mothers share a deep concern for their married daughters' health and welfare once grandchildren are in the offing. A pregnant woman is supposed to keep herself warm, to eat health food as prescribed by mama, to give up sports, work, parties, fun of any kind —"even Church choir! in fact all she wanted me to do was breed!" as the mother of a young family smiles about her mother.

Few young women give up work at first pregnancy, though in conservative families there is pressure on them to do so. Some eventually "drop out" when the second or third baby comes along and makes the double role of mother/worker too stressful; Malaysian fathers, though fond of their children, are not famous for domestic utility. But the wife's income is often needed, and so she slogs on at work and at home with such help as grannies and family members can give.

The majority of Chinese babies are born in hospitals, in rural areas they may be delivered by the district midwife. While the young mother is "in confinement", her mother or mother-in-law keeps up never-ending supplies of chicken soup stewed in distilled rice wine and herbs, *kachang ma*. This concoction is supposed to warm the new mother; it also keeps her mildly inebriated and therefore placid through the potentially turbulent post-natal depression period.

Family members and close friends visit the new mother with gifts of food; chickens to keep up the *kachang-ma* regime come in useful! Fruit are definitely OUT, granny will confiscate them on the grounds that they are "cold". Baby cards are not common, but if any are brought they must be free of storks. This bird resembles the heron, the Buddhist symbol of a pure soul occasionally featured at the funeral of a religious person; the association could put a newly delivered mother into hysterics! Flowers are unsuitable for the same reason — they belong to funerals. Gifts of money wrapped in red paper are acceptable, as are baby clothes (the mother was not supposed to make any while she was expecting) or, particularly if the infant is a boy, little items of gold.

While gender discrimination is not as blatant as it used to be, many Chinese families still prefer boy babies to girls. The theory, a leaky one in this age of social and geographic mobility, is that a boy will support his aged parents, while the expense of rearing a daughter will ultimately benefit her in-laws. Poor parents of many daughters sometimes give the latest female arrival for adoption, and "try again" for a boy who will save the family name from oblivion!

## Childhood

Chinese children are expected to make themselves useful from an early age. They help with farm and household chores, mind younger brothers and sisters, rub granny's legs and fetch and carry for mama. In coffee shops and groceries, quite young children can be seen serving customers, weighing, measuring, giving change.

The other side of this picture is the middle-aged spinster working on the family farm or in the shop, unpaid, deliberately kept unmarried, reserved for the duty of nursing her parents in their old age. After they have passed on, she will become The Auntie in one of her brothers' households. Admittedly, ex-officio aunties are becoming rarer as school attendance is made mandatory for both boys and girls, and society is learning to distinguish the institutionalized exploitation of an individual from filial piety.

Some Chinese families are in the habit of giving "medicine" to children regularly although they're perfectly healthy. It usually takes the shape of chicken broth stewed with many types of medicinal herbs; some are said to be cooling, others warming, some promote the child's teething, growth or eyesight. There's a herb for everything, never mind how it tastes; a good boy or girl swallows even a pungent or bitter concoction because "it's good for you" — and because he hopes it will be followed by a tidbit!

Many Chinese children are sent to kindergarten at the age of three or four. This is often pre-school in a very real sense: by the time they are five years old the little scholars know 20 to 50 basic characters, they do two-digit arithmetic, they have regular tests and exams to keep them up to the mark.

All Malaysian children start school after they have passed their sixth birthday. Chinese children may go to Malay-medium schools, but there is a network of Chinese-medium schools where the national language is taught as a subject, not as the medium of instruction. Proximity and the family's preference decide which school the child will attend. In Kuala Lumpur and a few other large towns, there are English-medium private schools, but these are very expensive and only cater for a tiny portion of the local population.

## Engagement and Marriage

The custom of arranging marriages for their unsuspecting offspring is all but obsolete among the Chinese community. Of course parents hope to influence their children, and will raise a ruckus if a patently unsuitable partner is introduced, but the days when a young man and maiden unquestioningly accept their family's choice are over.

There are commercial matchmaking agencies to help along shy people, but these are resorted to by persons seeking a partner themselves, not their families.

When a Chinese couple get engaged, the wider family must be notified and their approval sought. The parents make an announcement in the local press, "engagement sweets" are sent out to relatives and friends. These are tasty versions of peanut brittle and peanut toffee, several slabs of each packed in glossy red paper with the young couples' personal particulars on it in gold letters.

Sometimes the two sets of parents get together to discuss the financial implications of the intended match. What will the young woman bring by way of a dower? gold? jewels? a new car? Several changes of clothes for herself and her future husband are the traditional minimum, but in wealthy families large amounts of property may change hands.

The young man is expected to provide the house, and to make over land for his wife's maintenance if custom permits her to own any — in some Chinese communities land is only owned by males, and a widow is dependent on her sons' generosity and filial feeling for her maintenance.

The wedding date is fixed in consultation with a temple medium or an astrologer, often the same person. At the time of the engagement, the two young peoples' horoscopes were checked for incompatibilities; now is the time to choose the exact hour and minute of the wedding ceremony.

If the auspicious hour should be 02.17, the bride spends the whole evening and night getting dressed and plastered with wedding makeup, an art branch devoted to improving even a good-looking girl until her own mother hardly recognizes her! But the bride puts up with it all, knowing that, just like the bitter childhood medicines, "it's good for you". At 01.45 the bridal party set out to meet the groom at the clan temple. Luckily, only family and witnesses are expected to attend the marriage ceremony itself!

Wedding invitations are printed red on gold; these bid relatives and friends to one or more splendid banquets. The girl's family gives a going-away party for the daughter, the man's a welcome-to-the-fold one for the new bride.

Wedding banquets are usually held in the better restaurants, and they have to be lavish; people would talk if stint was shown on such an occasion. All that is good and expensive and rare is there, be it solid or liquid. Fine cognac flows in streams; the host family feels slightly embarrassed if none of their guests require at least a little assistance to get down the stairs and back to their cars after the party is over.

The commonest Chinese wedding present is an *ang pow*, a red packet containing money — a jocular saying has it that wedding invitations are "red summons", calling upon the guest to pay up!

The amount varies depending on the recipients' and the donor's social status; an elder uncle might contribute M$1,000 or more to a nephew's wedding, knowing that his brother will be obliged to return about the same amount when his sons get married. A middle-class guest, not a relative, would bring M$60, 80 or 100, the last gift being very generous. Note that the amount should be an even number, not odd — 30s and 50s are for funerals.

Wedding presents of the decorative and useful kind are also welcome. These should be colourfully wrapped, not in black-based paper however elegant, the colour of good fortune is RED.

Chinese couples get officially married at their Clan Association or in Church, or at the Registry Office. The tea-drinking rite may be carried out as a pleasant tradition, it is no longer valid to legalize a marriage. On the other hand, the respected relatives to whom the bride serves tea are more or less obliged to give her a present of gold...

A proper Chinese wedding is, first to last, an expensive exercise. Some working-class people practically exhaust their savings, or even borrow money, to satisfy the demands of tradition and the aunts.

The modern trend is, cautiously, towards the "mass wedding", a commercially organized occasion for 20 or more couples to exchange their vows. The number of guests is limited to 10 or 20 per couple, close relatives and best friends only. The distant cousins will grumble.

On the other hand, the venue for mass weddings is always some expensive hotel ballroom, splendidly decorated. The brides' lavish dresses, makeup and accessories are provided by the organizers. Glossy photos are taken, and the whole party flies off for a brief honeymoon in Thailand, Indonesia or Hong Kong, the sort of place the young couples have only dreamt of visiting. The whole thing is much more glamorous than they could have managed with their own means, yet considerably cheaper.

The unmarried career woman is slowly gaining acceptance in the Chinese community, but she is still a comparative rarity; families feel obliged to explain, apologize, or say that Mei Mei isn't married yet. In the old days, every expendable daughter was married off — dead or alive!

There used to be a provision for pairing off children who had died after their earliest infancy (when death was considered natural), either with each other or, in the case of girls, with a living husband. His existing wives probably took more kindly to a new co-wife who would only enter the family as a memorial tablet on the ancestral altar.

Ghost marriages were arranged to facilitate the deceased's entry into and maintenance in the other world. Unmarried persons may be reduced to the status of "hungry ghosts", sad spectres of those who die unknown and unmourned and have no descendants to care for their lonely graves. Childless couples adopted at least one son for the purpose of praying for them after their deaths.

If a son died unmarried, some conservative Chinese families

used to "adopt" not a son for themselves, but a son for the deceased. He was usually the child of poor parents, invested with his late "father's" family name and some presents from his bereaved grandparents, but left to live with his own family. On holidays and family feasts he visited his "grandparents" to pay his respects and receive a red packet. His function was to permit his late "father's" soul to enter heaven, which a man could only do if his son carried out the obsequies.

## Chinese Funeral

The Chinese take every care to bury their departed relatives with full ceremonial honours. This is for various reasons. One is that a hastily interred ancestor might decide that he had been insulted, and come back to haunt the family. Another is that in a close-knit community, people will talk. A family that dared to show stint on such an occasion would lose face! It is difficult to quote the price of "face"; an expert estimates that a first-class Chinese funeral including prayers, feasts during the mourning period and an adequate tomb costs about the price of a modest suburban bungalow.

A person may direct, during his lifetime, that his funeral be kept simple; this is considered a little eccentric but the wish will be respected. If the family is wealthy, they may make substantial charitable donations so face is preserved after all. "Grandpa didn't want us to splurge on last rites, but we are willing and able to spend money in his memory!"

After a person's death, the body is washed, dressed in several suits of clothing and wrapped in layers of silk gauze. Then it is placed in a coffin hewn from one trunk of hardwood, a very costly receptacle. Properly closed and sealed, this coffin may be kept in a house for as many days as it takes to organize the funeral and assemble the family without fear of embarrassing consequences. The astrologer may have a say, too. Embalming is not common in Malaysia except in the case of bodies that have to be transported long distances, and the practice of packing bodies in ice is almost unknown here.

Some families keep the body on a bier or bed for a couple of days and then coffin it; the clan association which acts as undertaker usually determines such details. In towns, it is unusual to keep a body for more than three days.

The coffin is placed in a prominent position, ceremonially screened off from view from the road or front door. Candles are lit, incense and paper "temple" money are burnt before it, the deceased's favourite possessions and refreshments, a comfortable chair, toilet implements are displayed near it. Everything is ready for his soul to come back and change, have a wash, smoke its favourite brand of cigar or enjoy a nip of cognac.

A coffin is never left unattended. Members of the family and the clan associaton sit around it day and night, eating and drinking and gambling. Prayers are said at certain times, music is played, young boys are paid to chant holy songs for the delectation of the body which must be addressed as if it was still alive.

Mourners and friends visit the house while the coffin is still there. The place has been taken over by the clan association, a crowd of roughly dressed, loudmouthed men which jar oddly with a foreigner's idea of undertakers! They serve tea or soft drinks to all comers, and escort them into the presence of the deceased.

Family members kneel and bow to the coffin, ordinary visitors just bow. This is expected of "outsiders" too; after all, if they weren't good friends they wouldn't call at such a time, and a good friend should show proper respect! Pregnant women do not visit a house of mourning. If a friend or a friend's relative has died, they can ring up the family and offer their condolences, explaining that they cannot attend in their present delicate condition. Children are not taken on condolatory visits either, though young relatives have to attend.

Presents of money are expected of relatives only, though a poor family is grateful for contributions from friends too. Wealthy families often request that donations be sent to the deceased's favourite charity. The important thing is that funeral donations must not be in multiples of 20 but consist of M$10, 30 or 50. Flowers are sent on the day of the funeral only so they will look fresh when they are piled on the grave.

The funeral procession leaves the house at a predetermined time, often 2 p.m. The immediate family are dressed in shapeless garments of unbleached calico, indigo or black cotton, depending on their generation status. Friends wear dull colours and no jewellery; red, pink orange and yellow are unsuitable funeral attire. Undertakers are everywhere, hollering and shouting, blowing whistles, marshalling everybody into proper marching order.

The hearse is preceded by lorries carrying banners of condolence from associations the deceased belonged to, by Buddhist monks or singers, the local drums-and-gongs ensemble and sometimes one or more brass bands. The hearse itself is a lorry, but for the first kilometre of the way it is driven at foot pace while 20 or 30 of the undertakers "pull" it along by calico strips. The chief mourner walks immediately behind, followed by relatives in their proper degrees.

The funeral procession of a prominent person can be very long and hold up all traffic for a couple of hours. In Malaysia's larger towns, corteges have to avoid the main streets; generally, after walking for about a kilometre, the mourners board waiting buses and travel to the cemetery or crematorium. Undertakers armed with whistles and flags direct traffic; it is not etiquette for other drivers to cut across a funeral procession or to overtake one.

The grave has already been dug after the directions of an expert geomancer. A wrongly aligned grandmother can cause no end of trouble! Mourners stand back while the coffin is lowered into the grave and then covered; they are served soft drinks and snacks by the indefatigable undertakers. As they are leaving the cemetery each mourner is given a new handkerchief with a red thread in it, two sweets tied with red thread, or simply a red thread; this must be waved over the left shoulder to prevent ghosts from following people home.

The bereaved family usually invites all mourners to a meal at the house after the interment. When returning from a funeral it is essential to take a bath and discard all clothes. They can only be worn again after a thorough wash.

A person who has been invited to a party on the same day that he has to attend a funeral must make up his mind which of the two is more important. The host at a convivial gathering, especially a wedding or birthday, will be upset if any of his guests come "fresh from a funeral" — they might bring along some of the bad luck that lingers after a visit to a cemetery and that a shower and a change of clothes cannot immediately efface.

The conservative family continues to mourn the deceased after the funeral. They wear black patches or black armbands with their sombre clothes. Prayers are read every evening until the seventh by Buddhist monks engaged for the purpose. On a set day the family visit the graveyard to set up the deceased's new establishment in the other world. He is provided with a grand house, a car (a Mercedes for preference), servants, a TV set and video player, all cleverly made of paper by specialists in the field. The things are burnt, together with millions of dollars in "temple money" (which costs a few dollars for a thick bundle of $100,000 notes!); the smoke rises to heaven where grandpa stands ready to receive the goods and put them to proper use.

The family is "in mourning" for a hundred days unless the deceased, during his lifetime, gave specific directions for a shorter period. While in mourning, close relatives may not wear colourful clothing, attend noisy parties, or get married.

At one time, mourning for a parent lasted three years; nowadays not all families observe even the hundred days. Young people refuse to be shackled by the bonds of tradition; once the funeral and seven days are over many resume their normal lifestyle and clothing.

## THE INDIAN COMMUNITY

Many Malaysian Indians entered the country during the last century. They were recruited as indentured labourers to work in the rubber plantations. Some have been here considerably longer; Islam is thought to have been brought to the Malay Peninsula by Indian traders who married into the various royal houses and achieved positions of great influence.

While most Malaysian Indians are Tamils from the southern part of the subcontinent, almost every linguistic group is represented here. The British brought in large numbers of clerical workers from Ceylon. Professionals, doctors and teachers from India came to work in Malaya after World War I and even later; many stayed. The Malayan Railways were practically run by Indians. Tall, bearded Punjabi policemen are the descendants of soldiers who arrived here nearly 200 years ago with the East India Company or the Colonial Armed Forces.

Today, there are Indians in all the professions and trades. Not many Malaysians have never been taught by an Indian teacher, treated by an Indian doctor or confounded by an Indian lawyer! At the other end of the scale, the Indian labourers in the rubber estates are among the poorest Malaysians.

## Clothes

Tamils traditionally wear a white garment resembling the *sarung,* the dhoti, and a white shirt. This is seldom seen on urban office workers but is worn when attending ceremonies.

Tamil women almost always wear the elegantly flowing sari, a six-metre length of fine cloth draped around the waist and tossed back over one shoulder. The torso is covered by a tight-fitting short-sleeved blouse called the "choli", a few centimetres of midriff are visible between its lower edge and the sari. Young Indian women usually follow the fashion trends of the day, though they will wear the sari for family visits or temple ceremonies. When doing house- or farmwork, Indian women often prefer to wear a *sarung* or slacks and blouse, more practical than the elegant but hampering swirls of sari.

An Indian woman with a red spot on her forehead or a red line in her hair parting is married. This red substance is *kumkum,* reddle saffron. Unmarried girls wear spots of any colour except red; a fashion-conscious young miss has enough pigments to match the shade of each item in her wardrobe!

A number of educated Indians are Christian. They keep some of their people's traditions, excluding of course the religious observances. The women may wear western dress or sari; the men usually opt for western outfits at work, though they like to relax at home in the Malay *sarung* — as indeed do lots of other Malaysians too!

Sikhs can be recognised from a distance by their tall stature topped by a turban. Many men still observe their religion's command concerning hair — it must not be cut. Moustache and side whiskers must not be trimmed either, but twisted sideways and then tucked under the edge of the turban. A boy's hair is tied up in a silk hankie on top of his head, as he grows to man's estate he starts to wear the soft cap and turban typical of his people. Some Sikhs have their hair cut and go "bareheaded" every day; for visiting the temple or conservative relatives they will always cover up.

Sikh women wear a trouser suit, the *salwar-khamis,* and a veil for outdoor wear. Styles range from baggy to slinky, fabrics from silks to handwoven cottons to the many man-made fibres available in Malaysia. The main thing is that the arms and legs are fully covered.

## Names

Each Hindu has his own individual name, with s/o (son of) or d/o (daughter of) to append the father's name. There are no surnames as the West knows them: the son of Ramesh s/o Savarimutu is not Sundralingam Savarimuthu but Sundralingam s/o Ramesh. Instead of s/o and d/o, the Malay abbreviations a/l (anak lelaki) and a/p *(anak perempuan)* are often used in official documents. If Shasheela d/o Manackavasigam marries Sundralingam s/o Ramesh, she will be know as Mrs Sundralingam or Madam Shasheela.

There are a number of Thomian Christian Indians in Malaysia. These people descend from ancestors who are said to have been baptized by St.Thomas the Apostle nearly 2000 years ago. They have biblical surnames like Abraham, John, Samuel, Jacob which are perpetuated in the family.

Some Indians have Portuguese names; these date back to the days when Goa, Ceylon, Malacca were colonies of Portugal. They have lived in Malaya for centuries and have become fully assimilated, like the Baba Chinese. Typical names are DeSilva, Rozario, SantaMaria, used as surnames from one generation to the next.

All Sikh men are known by a given name plus Singh. Singh is not strictly speaking a surname but a gender indicator, which Sikh names in themselves are not; Jagjit may be male or female until it appears as Jagjit Singh (man) or Jagjit Kaur (woman). A married

Sikh woman may be called by her own name, Surinder Kaur, or by her husband's, Mrs Sarjit. NOT Mrs Singh!

When speaking Malay, Indians like all other Malaysians are addressed as Encik for a man, Cik for an unmarried or Puan for a married woman. A person's occupation is often used as a form of address: *cikgu* (teacher), doctor, etc. The use of first names without some qualifying title means the two speakers are on very friendly terms; if they are related they use the status names proper to their degree. Indians call persons older than themselves "uncle" and "auntie" even if they are perfect strangers; this startles foreigners who are thus addressed by a shopkeeper.

## Religion

To expound Hindu theology would fill a book in itself, and one I am not qualified to write. Hindus revere a Supreme Being in many manifestations: male and female, benevolent and destructive. There is a Trinity of Brahma the Creator, Vishnu the Preserver and Siva the Destroyer, each with his consort or Female Principle. The same deity often combines negative and positive aspects within one personage.

The Lord Shiva who rides a bull is one of the chief gods, together with his consort Durga who bestrides a tiger. Between them the august couple symbolize creation, preservation and destruction — life and death. Hindu temples are dedicated to one or more main deities, but they are adorned with dozens, even hundreds of minor gods and goddesses, beautifully worked in the older shrines.

The Hindu scriptures are the Vedas, ancient writings that explain the mystery of life. From simply parables easily understood by the common people, the Vedas can be read and understood at the highest levels of abstract philosophy.

A Hindu household has a little altar where the housewife lights an oil lamp and presents offerings of flowers or fruits. Families or individuals visit the temple at any time they wish, though congrega-

*A Hindu temple and its pantheon of deities.*

tional prayers are usually held on Fridays. In the old days, the temple was about the only place young women were allowed to go to out of the house, and even then they would be carefully chaperoned.

Hindus are not allowed to eat beef; few take pork as it will render them unfit to enter a temple for six months. Milk products are an important part of the Hindu diet. About 10 per cent of Malaysian Indians are full vegetarians; some will not even eat eggs because an egg is a potential life. A number of others eat vegetarian food on Friday, the customary temple day, and on religious festivals.

Hindus believe in the reincarnation of the human soul. Their firm views on higher and lower forms of life are mirrored in the caste system which still obtains in India, though in Malaysia the edges have become much blurred. A person who lived a blameless life on earth will be born again as a good and wise human; a miscreant may come back as a frog or a cockroach!

The Sikh religion is an offshoot of Hinduism, started by a Punjabi warrior-scholar, Guru Nanak, in the 15th century. He abolished the caste system, and succeeding gurus created a powerful, disciplined state in the Punjab which resisted East India Company encroachments in the 18th century but eventually supplied some of the crack troops to John Company's armies. The tenth guru, Gobind Singh, instituted the rule that Sikh men must cover their unshorn hair with a turban, wear a pair of under-shorts and a steel bangle, carry a comb and a sword.

Practically all Sikhs, whether their hair is long or short, have a steel bangle on the right arm, and wear a turban at least occasionally. They presumably carry a comb; I have never seen one with a sword and this is not the place to discuss under-shorts.

## Festivals

Malaysian Indians celebrate various religious holidays, depending on their place of origin on the subcontinent. One of the most common is Deepavali, the Festival of Lights. There are many origin stories; one relates how the Lord Krishna killed the evil King Asura who had been tyrannizing his subjects. Deepavali symbolizes the triumph of light over darkness, good over evil.

Houses are cleaned, new clothes are made, many varieties of cakes and sweetmeats are prepared in readiness for the festival, which usually falls in October. At dusk, houses are decorated with dozens of lights; these may be electric "Christmas tree lights", earthenware or brass oil lamps. The mother of the house kindles the flames which twinkle through the darkness to welcome visitors.

The family rises before daylight. All take an oil bath, then dress in their best clothes and light the ceremonial lamps. Well-wishers turn up all day and continue coming until late into the night. They take off their shoes at the door, admire the display of fruits and flowers or the *kolam,* colourful floor-decorations of artistically sprinkled coloured rice grains, beans and pulses. The housewife and her daughters serve drinks and offer tray after tray of delicious, rich sweets and savouries.

In Malaysia, Deepavali is first and foremost a family festival, an occasion for Hindu Indians to welcome friends of other communities into their homes; Christian Indians have Open House at Christmas.

Deepavali is a private celebration; Thaipusam is a very public one. Dedicated to Lord Murugan, a god personifying the virtues of courage and endurance, this is a festival of thanksgiving for favours granted. Persons who have made a vow during the past year redeem it by carrying a *kavadi,* an ornamental load with two pots of milk or holy water dangling from both ends. This is attached to their bodies with steel spikes and hooks.

If this sounds gruesome, it is — to look at. Bare torsos are riddled with bells hooked into the skin; tall ornamented structures are skewered into brown muscular shoulders. Women carry the *kavadi* on yokes for reasons of modesty, some have their cheeks or tongues pierced by long steel spikes.

No person is permitted to carry a *kavadi* unless he has undergone the proper period of spiritual and physical discipline, training and fasting. At the time of the festival, participants are in a trance which leaves them awake and conscious but apparently dulls all feeling of pain.

Accompanied by music and chanting, the Thaipusam procession makes its way from a designated starting point to a shrine or temple. Worshippers and well-wishers line the route, singing and chanting, pouring water over the *kadavi*-carriers' feet. Once they arrive at the temple, the loads are unhooked from the devotees, the wounds rubbed with holy ash — and a few hours later not even scars remain!

## Childbirth

While his wife is in labour, a concerned Indian father stalks up and down the corridor with a good watch in his hand. The exact minute of the birth is vital information which the family astrologer will need to compute the child's horoscope.

Like all her Malaysian sisters, an Indian mother is kept in confinement by well-meaning elders. If the resident grandmother has her way, this lasts 16 or 31 days depending on the family's tradition. At the end of this period the baby is considered "safe", not likely to die in infancy; he is given a name by his father and presented to the family in a small party.

Friends may visit the new mother in confinement, bringing the usual sort of baby presents or small gifts of money. It is a good idea to ring up first and find out if the time is convenient. Some Indians consider certain days inauspicious for house visiting.

## Puberty Rites

Traditional Hindu families have a small celebration after a daughter's menarche. The girl is dressed in a new sari (she probably wore dresses until now) and made to sit between some of her married aunts. Purifying rituals vary from area to area, all cumulate in milk being poured over the girl's head and a lit lamp being put in her hand. Finally she is bathed in scented water.

Family members and close friends may be invited to witness this ceremony. They present the girl with gifts of gold jewellery or new clothes. This ritual makes the girl officially eligible for marriage.

## Marriage

A number of young Indians still contract arranged marriages, matches arranged for them by their parents. In the past, a Malaysian Indian

*A Hindu bride sits resplendent in her wedding outfit.*

might send his son's or daughter's horoscope and personal particulars to a respected matchmaker in "the old country". This professional then found a suitable marriage-partner based on astrological considerations.

A Malaysian under the age of 21 needs the parents' consent to marry, but the parents cannot make a son or daughter marry against their will. Some young people acquiesce to marriage arrangements; experts (in the form of elderly aunts) claim that arranged marriages are no less happy than love matches, and often more lasting! The normal thing is that the young man looks around, and informs his mother of a particular preference for this or that young woman.

Even if the young couple have found and chosen each other, a go-between has to "arrange the match" for the two sets of parents. Is this to discuss dowry arrangements? Up to a point, yes, though dowries are not the explosive issue here that they are in India. One of the go-between's duties is to ascertain that the two families are of compatible castes, and that the young couple's horoscopes match. He will consult the priest to choose an auspicious wedding date.

The wedding ceremony may be held at the bride's house or at the local temple, it usually depends where there is more room. The chanting and ceremonies can go on for hours, or be kept to a minimum. Much depends on the families' tastes and the priests' persistence.

The essentials of a Hindu wedding are that a sacred tree be planted for the couple by a happily married woman who has children, that the man's sash be tied to the woman's sari as they walk around the sacred flame, and that he tie the golden *thali* around her neck.

Wedding guests file past the couple, sprinkling yellow rice over them and dabbing sandalwood paste on their foreheads. The young woman now has a red spot on her forehead as a symbol of her new state, she wears jewellery on her head, neck, arms to signify joy and prosperity.

If the wedding is held at a temple, all guests have to leave their shoes at the doorstep. They may hand their presents to a family member; it is slightly more elegant to bring gifts to the house a day before the wedding. Money is an acceptable gift, but it should be an odd amount: M$ 31, 41, 61.

The wedding dinner is a triumph of the art of curry mixing. The guests are seated on the floor, the meal is served on banana leaves and eaten by hand. At a large wedding it may not be possible to ask for cutlery. The awkward eater may do well to bring along a spoon in a handbag. There is usually music during the dinner, possibly some dancers to entertain the company, but the guests just sit sedately and watch the performance.

In urban areas, the wedding breakfast is usually commercially catered, buffet-style. It is in the country, on plantations, that "banana-leaf weddings" may be enjoyed with all the traditional trimmings.

Sikh weddings are nearly always conducted at the temple. The bride, gorgeously dressed, is led into the groom's presence by her father or brothers — in the old days she used to be carried. The couple take their vows in front of a temple offical, and are then led around the Holy Book four times. The groom usually wears a suit and, of course, a turban. All male wedding guests have to have their heads covered too.

Catering in a Sikh temple is community work. A few stalwart men prepare huge tubs of *roti* dough to make a kind of pancake that is cooked on a griddle and eaten with the many delicious curries served up for the occasion. Meals at the temple, whether Sikh or Hindu, are always vegetarian.

## *Funeral*

When a person dies, as many relatives as possible have to be informed. The body is washed, dressed in new clothes and laid out. If the deceased was a married man, his widow used to be dressed in bridal attire as she sat beside his bed, silently grieving. This is no longer common; she usually wears the unadorned white of mourning while relatives pour in with condolences and offers of help.

As the body is carried out of the house, the widow's *thali* is removed from her neck by another widow. The newly bereaved takes off her finery and wedding sari if she is wearing it. She breaks her pretty glass bangles and dresses in white from then on; she will never wear jewellery again.

Hindus and Sikhs dispose of the dead by cremation though earth burial is also practised. In the major Malaysian towns there are crematoria; in "outstations" the open funeral pyre may have to be used. Women and children do not attend the cremation. They stay with the widow, to help her clean the house after the body has been removed.

## BUT WOULD YOU LET YOUR SISTER MARRY ONE...?

Malaysia has not got any spectacular race problems on its hands, maybe because the main groups keep by and large to themselves. There is a certain amount of intermarriage, and the foreign visitor is advised to be very, very cautious when discussing this "problem" with Malaysian acquaintances.

Young people of all races go to school and college together, how can they be prevented from falling in love with each other? They can't be; some Chinese families face the prospect of an Indian daughter-in-law with equanimity, others raise hell at first mention. This works vice-versa and in all combinations!

It doesn't have to be race. Any wealthy family may be horrified if their accomplished daughter brings home a labourer's son, their graduate son an uneducated girl, though they are of the same race and even distantly related.

But religion is the biggest problem here. A Muslim woman is not allowed, by religous law, to marry a non-Muslim man. A Christian, Buddhist, Hindu or Animist man will have to convert to Islam to marry his Malay sweetheart, and his family may take this in very bad part. A Muslim man can marry a Jewish or Christian woman but she will not be able to inherit his property after his death, nor be guardian of her own children; a Hindu, Buddhist or Animist girl will have to convert for his sake. Generally, Christians, Buddhists, Hindus and Animists can compromise among each other. Syaria religious law puts compromise out of a Muslim's personal power.

If such a "disaster" has happened in the family of your Malaysian friends, don't comment or congratulate them on their daughter's or son's engagement until they themselves mention the matter. (It could have been an elopement for all you know.) They may be delighted at the prospect of getting such a fine, worthy in-law and never mind religion. They may face the world with stiff upper lips — or they may be in despair, grieving over the "loss" of a beloved

135

child as if he or she had died. The last thing they want to hear are an expat's platitudes on Universal Brotherhood. What do YOU know about it?

Most families come round in the end. Grandchildren have almost miraculous powers of reconciliation. That's when you can come rushing in with congratulations, and a thumping baby gift to make up for the wedding present you never got round to giving.

## *Malaysians as Visitors*

The above notes give you some idea of what to expect when you visit Malaysian homes. You will of course want to invite Malaysians to your home, too. Giving dinners is fully discussed in the next chapter; but how do we handle the "just drop in!" situation?

As soon as people come up to the door, open it and invite them in. It is not polite to let people stand on the doorstep; don't holler: "It's open, just come in!" unless the visitor is a very close friend who drops in practically every day.

Your visitors will want to remove their shoes as they enter. Unless you have very strong objections to barefoot people in your house, let them.

Invite visitors to be seated and offer refreshments. This doesn't mean: "Do you want a drink?" They will modestly refuse such a blatant offer. Ask them if they would prefer a cool or a hot drink, orange or blackberry, or whatever choice there is.

Tea, coffee and orange drink are universally acceptable. Do not offer beer or other strong drink to Muslims; do not serve it to others if some of your guests are Muslim. In a large party this may be all right, in a small group it looks awkward.

If you serve tidbits, be sure they contain no trace of pork if one of your guests is Muslim. Refrain from serving minced-meat concoctions; you may know it's certified pork-free, your guests may not. Biscuits or cakes are usually safe with all comers.

If you have photo albums lying around in the room, your Malaysian guests will pounce on them with delight and examine them frame by frame. You will be asked to comment on the more interesting photos like Aunt Ethel on skis in Grindelwald, grandpa's prize tulips, or that dreadful shot of yourself at nine...

Keep albums out of reach if you don't like such well-meaning curiosity.

Do not let your dog snuffle visitors, or go anywhere near them, if they are Muslims. A dog's inquisitive nose is as unclean as the rest of the animal. Tie him up if he's too friendly for his own good.

Cats are all right, so are toddlers and small children; most Malaysians like children, and don't resent their pranks and noise. In addition, children may prove valuable ice-breakers if the conversation started a bit stiffly.

# Chapter Seven

# LAND OF
# A THOUSAND TASTES

"Malaysians are always eating!" complains an expatriate here — or
was he exulting?

Malaysians don't actually eat more than other people, but they
eat often, in small amounts. Most people have coffee or tea at home
in the early morning. By 10 a.m. they're feeling peckish again.
Clustered around roadside stalls and coffee shops they're sampling
"snacks". This wonderfully all-inclusive term covers breakfast,
brunch, late lunch, early afternoon tea, tea-dinner, "I'm not actually
hungry" dinner, supper, and the refreshments revellers need on their
way home from a party at 3 a.m.

Quite apart from what mama cooks — she cooks regularly and amply — there is always some tasty food just waiting to be eaten somewhere. And you can trust Malaysians to know where.

## FOOD STALLS

Malaysians get their insatiable reputation from the numerous food stalls here. The climate permits open-air eating all the year round, without discreet restaurant walls that shelter the gourmet and the gourmand in colder countries!

A mobile food stall is carried on a yoke. Some quite elaborate dishes can be prepared by a man who brings along his portable grill or clay stove, a supply of foodstuffs, bowls, spoons, plates and wrapping materials.

A little booth on wheels is the next step up. Its owner has a stove and storage shelves built into the wagon, he may even carry half a dozen rickety stools so his guests can sit down while they enjoy his wares.

In every nook and corner of town, along bus stops, in parking lots, stalls flourish like mushrooms after the rain. Built of discarded packing materials, plywood, mat roofs, few of them have licences. Each time the municipal authorities feel the urge of public hygiene upon them, illegal stalls are outlawed. Dismantled within a few hours they vanish, only to spring up again in another spot, or in the very same location after the sanitary zeal has been redirected at stray dogs, spitting in public thoroughfares and overflowing rubbish bins.

There are quite a lot of licenced food stalls. These are little houses, sometimes actually inhabited by the stallkeeper; they are built of timber planks and tin roofing, firmly padlocked when not open for business.

Every street in town has one or more coffee shops, and almost every coffee shop has food-stall tenants. The restaurant serves coffee, tea and other drinks; the food stalls offer noodle dishes, dumplings, rice porridge, meat or vegetarian soups, griddle cakes with curry sauce, whatever could possibly tempt the appetite for a substantial second breakfast.

Open-air stalls are for the eat-and-run crowd. The coffee shop is the breakfast location of choice for people who like to linger over their coffee, read the newspaper, meet friends who share their predilection for the town's best *laksa* or whatever the favourite dish is. Small-time businessmen even use the local coffee shop as an informal office.

A number of downtown shopping malls have hawkers' centres for the delectation of their patrons, often in the basement. They offer all the variety of an outdoor market, they are usually cleaner, and they are air-conditioned.

A distinction is made between Chinese stalls or coffee shops, and Malay or Indian ones. The former serve all types of food including pork, the latter only serve *halal* (kosher) dishes. Some Indian stalls specialize in vegetarian food, a taste revelation to the expat used to textured soy proteins flavoured to imitate meat!

In a market with lots of food stalls, customers are expected to choose the side they wish to patronize and eat there. It would be uncouth, and unwise, to stroll among the Muslim shops munching a pork-filled dumpling. In fact, few Malaysians eat food while walking about; only small children run around while sucking ice creams or baby bottles filled with orange drink.

## What is Served in Stalls?

First of all, drinks. The climate makes it essential that enough liquid be consumed; an army of hawkers devote their efforts to making this liquid available. Boxed or bottled drinks with straws are sold everywhere. If the buyer wants to take a bottled drink with him, he can choose between paying for the bottle deposit as well, or having the contents decanted into a plastic bag. This is looped to a string, a straw is inserted, and he can take it back to his car, or office, or wherever.

Some drinks stalls have a quaint-looking wrought-iron ice shaver; this is for cooling beverages. A glass or bowl is filled with shaved ice, and the drink or sweet soup poured over it. Some quite remarkable concoctions, called "chendol", are prepared of boiled red or green beans, green bean flour "worms", maize corns, irish moss jelly, gingko nuts — the list is endless, the possible combinations without number. All or any of the above are spooned over shaved ice, the mound is sweetened with flavoured sugar syrups and a dash of condensed milk or coconut cream.

The newcomer to Malaysia is not advised to try any shaved-ice dishes until he has had time to get used to our multifarious germs. Bottled or boxed drinks are safer in the first few weeks!

Hawkers' centres have one or several coffee and tea stalls. Water is freshly boiled for each cup of beverage so the germ problem does not arise. Some Indians specialize in the preparation of *teh tarik,* "pulled tea": the cook has made a cup of tea in the usual way and added milk and sugar. To completely blend the liquid, he pours it from one container into another three or four times. The arm with the full mug is flourished high above his head, the stream of tea gushes into the other mug held at thigh level. To an unbiased observer, *teh tarik* is strong tea with milk and sugar, though devotees affirm that it tastes much, much better. I suspect that the fun of watching, the ever-present hope that one day he'll miss and pour a cup of scalding tea into his apron pocket, adds to the enjoyment!

Many stalls sell what is innocently called "cakes". A large number of cakes are savouries, with or without meat, most of them deep-fried. Red-hot cornish pasties are called curry puffs. There are spiced muffins, spring rolls in many flavours, rice or yam slice topped with fried chili, onions and spices.

Traditional sweet cakes are based on glutinous rice or rice flour, not baked but steamed. One kind is prepared in large trays, topped with coconut cream and cut into bite-sized squares. Another is

*A teh tarik man doing his thing.*

rolled of rice flour mixture, filled with palm sugar or bean paste and steamed on banana leaf circles, yet another packed in little "crates" made of a fragrant leaf. One beautifully sticky confection is tossed in grated coconut, giving it the appearance of a pale green snowball. These rice cakes are highly coloured, making the traditional cake stall look like a jewel display.

When ordering food, it is advisable to watch the cooks at work first. It is all right to point at the supplies, and order "one of this". If customers at a neighbouring table are eating something that looks promising, ask for "one of that", only you must not point at people.

Indicate the dish with a very discreet gesture of thumb over loose fist, or with a glance; discuss your query with the stallkeeper in a low, confidential voice.

When dishing up, the stallkeeper serving an expat may hesitate over the spices and sauces. If you don't like your food hot, say "No chili!", he'll get the message. Hot condiments are sometimes served separately. Indicate the blobs of goo in extra dishes, or on the side of your plate, and ask: "Chili?"

Pasta in a myriad forms, known as "mee", is common stall food. Rice or wheat flour spaghetti, vermicelli, noodles and squiggles are cooked in soup, dry, or fried; they are garnished with meat or vegetables, flavoured with curry sauces or floating in meat stock.

The Indian answer to pasta are griddle cakes, generally called *roti,* which come lean or fat, plain or filled, dumpy or flaky. They may be served with lentil or pea curry dip as a snack, or as the base on which an elaborate meal is served. Many Malaysian Indians eat *roti* as their daily staple, in preference to rice; it is not only stall food!

*Sate,* skewered grilled meat, is a Malay and Indonesian specialty. There is a *sate* man in every village. He mounts a charcoal grill on the back of his bicycle and makes daily rounds, setting up shop to toast a few dozen sticks to smoky perfection wherever customers stop him. In hawkers' centres he sets up his grill near the edge and trusts to the fragrance wafting across the seated crowd to attract customers.

Some food stalls in coffee shops offer a limited variety of very delicious, artistically finished Chinese "cakes" called "dim sum". *Dim sum* is the sort of snack that can degenerate into a meal. It is usually served on little plates containing three tidbits of the same kind.

*Dim sum* are best enjoyed by a group of friends. Each orders his one or two favourites. Once the table is covered with dumplings and rolls and stuffed mushrooms and puffs and spiced spare ribs,

*A vendor fans the ubiquitous* sate *which is eaten accompanied with spicy peanut sauce and* ketupat, *cubes of compressed rice cooked in coconut leaf.*

Dim sum, *the traditional Chinese lunchtime or brunchtime feast, is served piping hot in small servings.*

sharing and barter-trading starts. In the coffee shops most *dim sum* contain pork; a few of the better hotels offer pork-free *dim sum* luncheons on a Sunday. Some Chinese restaurants feature this specialty in a big way: trolleys laden with up to 20 different kinds circle among the tables, gourmets select, eat, select more while a waitress refills their tea bowls. The bill is computed according to a census of the empty serving dishes — and it may be hefty. But a good *dim sum* spread is worth good money.

Besides snacks, food stalls also serve quite substantial meals. The most common is the world's original takeaway, *nasi lemak* ("buttered rice"): A scoop of rice is garnished with spicy *sambal,* fried dried anchovies and peanuts, half a boiled egg and a few slices of cucumber, and is wrapped in a large leaf. This sort of package used to be taken along on jungle foraging expeditions, school picnics, community work parties, political campaigns. Budget-conscious office workers buy a package of *nasi lemak* and a packaged drink from the food stall downstairs and have lunch at their desks. The large leaf has been replaced by a sheet of plastic of late, but the contents are as good as what mama used to make.

*Nasi campur* is a more elaborate version of *nasi lemak,* a packet or plate of rice with a selection of cut meats. Watch the stallkeeper at work while he hacks roast chickens and ducks with a razor-sharp cleaver, and take heed: the meat is cut straight across, leaving all the vitamins and proteins *and* bone splinters lurking for the hasty eater!

Many coffee shops serve a Malaysian variant of fast food. A dozen or more meat, vegetable and fish dishes are kept hot in stainless steel containers. Each customer gets a plate full of steaming rice, then he chooses a ladleful of this, that and the other main course. This type of canteen is catching on in the bigger towns where people don't go home for lunch; strolling tourists may like to drop in for a taste of typical home-style cooking in these places.

McDonald, Kentucky and similar Western fast-food chains are making an impact on the Malaysian food scene. The clientele is overwhelmingly young. School-age youngsters like the colourful with-it decor, the noisy music, the exotic food "just like the kids in TV serials eat!", and the comparative freedom they enjoy in a place shunned by middle-aged aunts. To cater for local tastes, chili sauce stands beside the tomato. Curry pizzas are served besides the traditional tomato-and-cheese combinations — but there's no bacon or ham, for these places are *halal,* permitted to Muslims. Many people refer to hamburgers as "beefburgers" just to make the point that there is no pork in the patties!

## FOOD TABOOS

It is generally known that Muslims don't eat pork, a meat declared *haram* (forbidden) by their religion. The restriction doesn't end there, however. Animals have to be slaughtered in a particular way to make the meat *halal,* fit for Muslim consumption. Expatriates have to remember this when inviting local guests to a meal.

All beef and mutton sold in Malaysian wet markets and supermarkets is *halal,* even if it is imported. Packaged frozen chickens are usually *halal* too. Some housewives buy live fowls in the market and slaughter them at home to ensure really fresh meat. Few foreign householders share this preference; those who do should ask a Muslim to kill any chickens that will be served to Muslim guests. For a small tip, a driver or gardener will usually oblige.

Hindus and Sikhs are not permitted to eat beef; some will eat chicken, goat and mutton, some only chicken; of course all are free to enjoy fish. Fish and marine products are not restricted for most Malaysians except vegetarians. Hindus may eat pork, but few do it.

Vegetarian Hindus use pulses, legumes and milk products to obtain the necessary proteins. Strict Chinese Buddhists usually refuse eggs, and don't like cheese or curd; their proteins are derived from soy and other beans, and gluten washed out of wheat flour.

Indian and Chinese vegetarian cooking are two sciences well worth learning. There are vegetarian restaurants in town; this may be the place to give a bit of deserved publicity to clay-pot beancurd, a melt-in-the-mouth combination of plumply fried beancurd nuggets, choice vegetables and mushrooms simmered in an earthenware pot. Another favourite is chick-pea curry with quail eggs, or bite-sized chunks pulled off *roti chanai* and dipped in lentil curry. And ...and...and...

It is perfectly in order to ask people: "Is there any food you don't take?" when inviting them to dinner. If you consider this too blatant, try: "I'm planning to roast a leg of lamb — or would you prefer something different?" If they are vegetarians they'll speak up. Ask prospective guests if they like cheese before building up a whole meal around a huge cheese soufflé. Some Asians like cheese, some tolerate it, some can't stomach it. Literally so: people who ingested no further milk products after being weaned develop lactose intolerance, so milk products will make them sick!

Consider well before inviting vegetarians to a mixed dinner party. Some are quite happy with having a special dish served up to them, others find the presence of meat-eaters at table distasteful. Strict vegetarians of strong views don't usually accept dinner invitations anyway; neither do conservative high-caste Hindus whose food needs to be cooked in pure brass pots.

## MALAYSIAN CUISINES —SOME POINTERS

Most Malaysians eat rice at least once a day. This grain is the staff of life; other foods are eaten "to give flavour to the rice."

Much of Chinese food is stir-fried in the wok or *kuali,* the wide shallow pan that serves 101 purposes in the hands of a skilful cook. Vegetables are usually just done, with a crisp crackle left in them; a frugal housewife will cut meat into small bits and use them to add savour to vegetable dishes. Fish can be fried, steamed or even smoked in the *kuali.* Soups are substantial, making use of "everything but the squeak" of meat and bones bought in the market.

Malay food is always well done, nearly all meats and many

vegetables are curried in a variety of flavours. A careful housewife mixes her own curry spices: this is an art amounting to a science, and took her years to learn! Turmeric adds colour and a slightly bitter taste, cloves and anise are sweet; chili and pepper put the heat into the gravy; cumin and caraway smooth a rough mix; fenugreek, the spice much overused in commerically blended curries, gives just a hint of pungency. And so forth, and so on...the symphony is completed with the addition of coconut cream and an acidifier, usually tamarind (*asam paya*) or *asam gelugor*.

*Nonya* is an ancient, long-perfected hybrid of Malay and Chinese cooking. The word means "lady" in Malay, but in Malaysia it refers to the wife of a "Baba", a Straits Chinese whose ancestors came to Malacca three or four hundred years ago.

The Babas and Nonyas have become fully assimilated in their new home country. They speak a dialect of Malay with chunks of Hokkien in it; few of them are literate in Chinese though many used to be educated in Malay, and kept diaries or wrote poems and romances in Jawi! Their housewives have mastered the art of spice blending, of simmering and braising and roasting and steaming. They took to *belachan* and chili and tamarind and coconut cream as to the manner born; their cuisine is distinguished from the Malay only by its use of pork.

Chinese, Malay and Nonya cooking are liberally garnished with a fermented prawn paste, known as "belachan" in Malaysia and "trasi" in Indonesia. For people who like it, *belachan* tastes pungent; to others it smells putrid and they wouldn't want to taste it thank you!

*Belachan* is pounded with chili, garlic and other spices in the heavy stone mortar found in every Malaysian kitchen. It may be enjoyed as a dip for blanched vegetables, or fried and used to season vegetable or fish dishes.

Eurasian cuisine is an extension of Nonya into the realm of the Portuguese and the Indian. Its most distinctive dishes are the "devil curries". No sensible explanation for this name can be given, though the novice who burns his mouth on one may start to suspect...

Devil curries don't use coconut cream but are completed with the addition of vinegar. Pork and ham are meats commonly "devilled" to tender perfection in a tangy, hot-sour sauce that is quite dark in colour. They're certainly one hell of a treat!

## RESTAURANT EATING

Chinese home-cooking is economical. Restaurant food just has to be lavish.

The reason for inviting people out is nearly always to celebrate something, at least to demonstrate the host's generosity. If anything was less than perfect, he would lose face!

A Chinese restaurant that wants to keep its regular customers and their faces employs a team of highly skilled cooks. A festive dinner consists of lots of meat, different meats imaginatively dressed. It is possible to sit through a seven-course meal and eat seven meat dishes with a mere sprinkling of vegetables and maybe a parting shot of rich fried rice or noodles!

Guests invited to a Chinese dinner are met by their host in the foyer of the restaurant. He welcomes them and has them ushered into the room where his wife is presiding over a festively decorated table. She orders drinks — preferably fine spirits or beer. Soft drinks will be provided for those gauche enough to ask for them, but the non-drinking connoisseur's beverage is Chinese tea.

Pre-dinner small talk covers the usual topics of the day. If a menu card is tucked somewhere among the floral arrangements, the dinner may be enjoyed in anticipation. Even if it is written in Chinese, the number of lines indicate the number of courses you will have to ration your appetite for. Ask a neighbour to translate, compliment the hostess on the bounty of her choice. She will smilingly deprecate the poor food — only seven courses — very limited selection — hopes her friends will forgive her husband's audacity in inviting them. Some of the guests get a lot of fun out of complimenting as extravagantly as the poor lady apologizes. What's a party without party games?

Diners are usually punctual. By seven-thirty the host enters, accompanying the last arrival. The waitress clears the table of useless extras like flowers and starts loading the round expanse with food. Now we get down to business!

The hors d'oeuvre is often a "cold dish", artistically arranged cold cuts of many kinds, some of them quite unrecognizable to the novice. A foreign guest can do his host and dinner companions no greater favour than to ask, ask, ask! and of course eat, eat, eat! There is no worse damper to the party mood than a chap who sits there glowering at the bits and pieces on the serving dish, gingerly picking up a slice of chicken and a sprig of parsley and politely muttering "fine, fine" when asked how he's enjoying the meal.

What looks like pale meat loaf may well be soy protein, or fish "cake". Those squiggly transparent strips in the centre are jellyfish. The black translucent egg is 100-year egg, the slices of radish next to it are shaved preserved ginger. You may not want to eat heartily of all the above, but taste them, ask about them. Try anything once; just don't ask about the traditional recipe for preserving those black eggs...

The host may consider it his duty to load an honoured guest's plate with choice morsels. He will transfer them with his chopsticks; this sounds rather unhygienic, but it is not. Food is taken off the chopsticks with the lips, the sticks themselves are not put into the mouth.

Chopsticks are the correct way of eating a Chinese dinner, though any guest will be given a spoon and fork. In some restaurants all foreigners are considerately issued with their familiar tools; if they want chopsticks they have to request them!

I never fail to admire the Chinese diner who can pick up a chicken leg with his chopsticks, gnaw the meat with relish, and finally lay down the clean bone with his chopsticks! Not everybody is up to this dexterity. If chopsticks become inadequate, the porcelain spoon or even a daintily plied pincer of fingers may help. As long as it is neatly done and the fingers are not licked, it's not bad manners; neither is placing bones, fish tails and other discarded inedibles on the tablecloth.

There's a reason why the cautious guest ascertains the number of dishes before setting out. The novice used to a standard three-course dinner followed by coffee and cigars tucks heartily into the cold dish, the roast chicken, the yam basket filled with fried cashews and fried meatballs; the salt-baked prawns don't go down so smoothly; the beancurd mushrooms stick in his throat; the steamed fish looks and even smells distinctly fishy; as for the herb-steamed chicken, nothing anybody can tell him of its medicinal and digestive properties will help him swallow a spoonful. The Chinese Have a Word for It, and so do the English: He's eaten too much.

And he hasn't been confronted with the dessert yet! It may be fresh fruit, a welcome end to an over-rich meal; it may be iced tinned fruit with squares of almond jelly floating in the syrup. Butter-fried pancakes oozing a delicious high-calorie sweet bean paste are another favourite, or candied bananas dredged in sesame seeds and cooled to crispy crackling point in iced water.

As above, The Chinese Have a Word for It!

Indian and Malay dinners are more predictable in that the main courses are usually served up together. Talk about a groaning table. One reason why festive dinners in a traditional Malay setting are served on mats on the floor is probably because no table could hold all the bounty.

At an Indian feast, guests are served a plate on which a *roti* is spread like a doily; they tear off shreds of this fine bread and use it to pick and dip the many curry, roast meat, vegetable and relish dishes spread temptingly all over the table. It is all right to use spoon and fork, but the correct way to eat an Indian dinner is by hand even if the staple is rice.

Malay meals should also be eaten by hand, but let the novice beware! it looks easy, but is quite tricky to do daintily. The thumb and three fingers of the right hand only are used, and they must not get greasy above the second joint. Nobody flickers an eyelid if a foreign guest manages to coat his whole fist with curry gravy, but the women in the kitchen will chuckle over the dishwashing: "Ate like a small child, he did — you should have seen his greasy paw!"

## *FOOD FOR THE ADVENTUROUS*

Eating unfamiliar food can and should be an adventure. Few people who trembled and shrieked through "Jaws" have any idea how tasty shark's fin soup or omelette can be; it would be a shame if the great white killer put them off trying. After all, the fact that a bull can kill a matador doesn't put us all off beefsteak.

The oddest foods served up in Malaysia, and some of the most expensive, are what may be loosely termed marine freaks. Besides shark's fin and jellyfish, there is bêche-de-mer, "sea-cucumber" to quote a literal-minded person who doesn't care for the swabbly sausage-shaped objects. Frogs' legs are air-flown in from East Malaysia and even Taiwan, which should give an indication of their price and status. Then there are turtles' eggs, costly because their producers face extinction; this explains why turtle soup is usually a clandestine treat, very expensive indeed.

Shellfish of all kinds and sizes are found in the shallow waters around the Malaysian coast. Clams, cockles and mussels are familiar to most people. A trumpet-shaped sea snail may be a novelty. Its pointed end is knocked off before cooking, and the diners suck the mollusc out of the mouth of the cone with much lusty hissing. Another shellfish resides in what resembles a 2.5 centimetre length of bamboo. The most expensive shellfish going is abalone, most of it imported from Korea, Japan and China. This high-priced delicacy of rubbery texture and little flavour adds definite tone to a meal —

*Durian, the Malaysian king of fruit, is a local favourite. Either you love it or you hate it, but you can't ignore it.*

if it's dear it MUST be delicious.

Another Malaysian delicacy costs up to M$400 per 100 grammes and it isn't even rubbery — just tasteless. This is the famed bird's-nest for which Chinese traders braved the South China Sea in their cockleshells of junks in the 8th century.

Bird's-nests are made by a type of swiftlet, the *collocalia fuciphaga,* out of saliva, twigs and dirt. After an elaborate cleaning process, the nests are sold in small amounts for medicinal or ostentatious purposes. They are cooked in soup, but what gives this dish its flavour is the chicken that is cooked along with the nests, the vegetables that are simmered and finally pureed into the broth. Bird's-nest can also be made into a drink, sweetened with rock sugar. A blade of screwpine leaf will give some taste to this insipid concoction, though many Chinese swear by its efficacy in curing grandma's cough and grandpa's grouch.

Bird's-nest is, strangely, sold by Chinese herbalists as a herb. So are a wide assortment of woodchips, seeds, pips, roots and barks and dried frog. And, as an afterthought, dried herbs.

Many Chinese dinners feature a chicken soup with herbs as the second-last course. This is a discreet aid to the diners' digestion. Many herbal mixtures are prescribed and made up by housewives who swear by the curative or preventative powers of their favourite concoctions.

Some simple combinations are sold in the wet markets and supermarkets. These are tasty and harmless, but the lay person is not advised to meddle deeply with actual medicines. A Chinese physician or herbalist has studied for many years before he reached proficiency. Some of the substances in the shelves and glass jars of the Chinese pharmacy are potent stuff!

## FOREIGN GUESTS IN A MALAYSIAN HOME

Urban Malaysians do not invite people to their homes for meals very often. While friends drop in on each other for informal chats and afternoon teas, people are more likely to entertain in restaurants. If there is reason for a feast — a wedding, a birthday, the safe return of a family member from abroad, recovery from an illness, a funeral anniversary — they handle it with aplomb. But to be invited to a meal by a middle-class Malaysian family is a special compliment, and their foreign friends should esteem it as such.

Guests should arrive within half an hour of the stated time, not later. You will be met by the host or hostess at the door and (probably) asked not to take your shoes off. If nobody else is wearing theirs, make a nice remark about walking on carpets with bare feet and take yours off too; if the others are wearing theirs, leave yours on.

A guest is not expected to bring a gift, but something small is always appreciated — flowers, nicely packed sweets for the children, a souvenir from your own country. Hand this to the hostess soon after arriving. If there are small children in the house they will probably clamour for it to be opened, otherwise it is etiquette to put it aside after polite thanks.

The guests will be seated in the lounge and served with drinks and tidbits. If the host's parents are present, spend at least some time conversing with them even if there are language difficulties.

The meal is likely to be served buffet-style. The hostess asks the women to start; they insist they couldn't possibly precede her; after some polite skirmishing the eldest woman present usually sets a good example for the others to follow.

In a conservative household, the men may be served separately from, and before, the women. This is not the time to demonstrate your firm opinions on the equality of the sexes. In your own household you set your own standards; as a guest you have to honour your host's.

If the party is small, the meal may be served at the table; these arrangements depend on how many willing helpers there are in the kitchen. Sit-down dinner makes for a cosy atmosphere and animated conversation, and gives the hostess a better chance to enjoy the party. During a buffet, the dear lady is apt to be hovering anxiously among the guests, urging each who's half-cleared his plate to go for seconds.

Some Malaysian families serve coffee after a dinner party, others don't. Be prepared for a minor shock: the brew may be ready-sweetened.

Unlike a dinner party in a restaurant which breaks up after the last dish has been consumed, guests in a private home linger after the meal. If the invitation was for eight p.m. and the meal was served at nine, the party wouldn't be expected to break up until eleven. It is usually one of the more senior guests who gives the signal. "This was a wonderful dinner, Frank and Molly, but it's getting past my bedtime!" is one way of putting it; everyone else consults their watches, is amazed how quickly time has flown, but unfortunately tomorrow is a working day...

Thank-you notes dispatched the morning after a private dinner party are not the Malaysian norm, but they are hugely appreciated as a rarity. Take the trouble to send one and you'll rise in everyone's estimation!

## MALAYSIAN GUESTS IN AN EXPATRIATE HOME

Once you are settled and have acquired a circle of local friends, you will want to entertain them in your home, too. This requires neither great preparation nor huge expenses, just some consideration and tact.

Plan the menu to cater for religious sensibilities. If any of your guests are Muslim, don't include any but *halal* foods; if one is Hindu, don't cook beef. Chicken and fish are meats acceptable to all.

Consider whether your guests have been abroad, or frequently mix with foreigners, before laying out a battery of glasses and six forks at each setting. Beyond a doubt this looks impressive, but in western-style dining there is such a thing as Using the Wrong Fork, and your guest may be too anxious about etiquette to enjoy what's served up on a succession of warmed bone-china plates!

Nobody appreciates a formal western dinner more than Malaysians who are used to this sort of thing, though you have to cut out the wines if your guests are Muslim.

A buffet dinner will put your Malaysian friends at ease. Unless you have perfectly trained servants, it will be less of an ordeal for them, too!

What sort of foods should you cook? Many Malaysians look forward to a meal in an expatriate household because they hope to taste "something different". As you have already eliminated what people can't eat (forbidden meats, possibly cheese), give them some of your own country's special dishes if the ingredients are available here. One dish of rice should be available for those who can't manage without, but many of your local friends will tuck into potato salad, mash, garlic bread, risotto, Italian-type pasta with relish.

Most Malaysians wax lyrical over western desserts. This is your chance to shine! Local sweets are on the whole stodgy rice-flour puddings; amaze guests with a Pavlova, a trifle, a full-dress fruit salad, or your very own chocolate confection. (The outstation resident has to buy cream on her trip to a bigger town.)

Some hostesses make one sweet dish with liqueur or sherry and one without; this gives teetotallers a choice. Hot sweets are appreciated as a novelty, though the climate seems to cry out for something cold.

Sometimes Malaysians offend their hostess unwittingly by asking her, in tones of utter disbelief: "You mean, you cooked all this? You *yourself* cooked it?" A few ignorant souls still labour under the prejudice that All Europeans are Rich, therefore No European Women Are Capable of Doing Anything Useful. Bite down the sharp retort that rises to your tongue and chat about your home and background, charmingly. Tell them how your mother taught you to cook, but of course there is also domestic science in school...for boys as well as girls.

This approach treats her remark as a compliment (which it was in a flabbergasted way). In giving your mother and your school credit, however, you're modestly turning it aside. Face is saved all around, and let's hope that the lady never asks such a question again.

## SHOPPING FOR FOOD

In the smaller Malaysian towns, the obvious place to shop for vegetables, fish and meat is the wet market. The wet market belongs to the town centre. It is often near the riverside which was the lifeline of traffic in the old days, when fish was landed straight from the boats and farmers brought their produce from their upriver vegetable patches.

Kuala Lumpur has several wet markets, but urban geography and traffic conditions make it impractical for most housewives to

157

*An open-air market where fresh produce is sold daily.*

visit one daily. The neighbourhood shopping centre has taken over, and the Van Man.

A number of enterprising business men cruise the major town's residential areas during the morning hours, selling provisions. They have been to the wet market at the crack of dawn and chosen what their clientele needs: fresh meat and fish, vegetables, preserved foodstuffs, condiments, eggs. Some van men also bring bread, though a baker's van is likely to cruise the streets with a fragrant load of fresh baked goods.

Each van has its fixed route, its fixed stops; the driver will attend a good customer separately if she prefers the privacy of her own front drive. Most housewives like to walk a few houses for community shopping and a little chat with their neighbours. In urban housing areas, where neighbourliness is not a conspicuous virtue, many women at least know each other from their van meetings.

The van man is also a newsmonger of sorts. An SOS-call for domestic help may be put out through his agency, an appeal for the return of a strayed cat or an escaped canary. Many families leave the daily shopping to their helpers, so the "amah network" is maintained by the van man too.

If no van man calls in your area, or if you find him unsatisfactory, try the neighbourhood shopping centre. It has several groceries, one or more of which also sell fresh foodstuffs. Then there may be a small supermarket that stocks frozen produce and some imported foods of the kind you like.

The big supermarkets in the urban centres sell a wide variety of foodstuffs, local and imported. Fresh vegetables and meats, neatly packed in plastic, are more expensive than in the market, but the busy working wife who does her shopping in the lunch hour finds supermarkets a boon.

## MALAYSIAN COOKING FROM A TO Z

Casting an eye over the van man's supplies, scrutinizing the offer at the neighbourhood store, taking in the plethora of edibles available in the bigger wet markets may throw up the question: What are all these things? Some you can easily recognize. Others you couldn't even classify as animal-mineral-vegetable!

Shopping with a local friend will add to your general knowledge in the edibles department. The best way to learn about curry pastes is to follow an Indian women who chooses the supplies for her own kitchen; only a Chinese or Nonya mother can really guide you around those herbs that will keep your family free of snuffles, tummy aches and bad temper. To learn to choose the right fish for the right purpose, follow your Malay friend to the fish market and watch her deal with both the produce and the dealers.

Many expatriate women take cooking courses while they are

here. These are an excellent opportunity to learn what's what in the wet market, and what to do with it once it reaches the kitchen. Some canny housewives also send their household help for such courses. Most local girls are competent home cooks, but few are skilled at the preparation of specialty dishes. For an uninterrupted supply of gourmet food from your own kitchen, educate the cook. This will also improve her employment opportunites after you have left Malaysia — not, let's hope, before.

If you only have time for one course, I'd recommend Nonya. This cuisine has "a little bit of each" from each Malaysian community and uses all kinds of foodstuffs found on earth, in the air and in the sea. And if others there be, the Nonyas know where to find them, buy them at the cheapest rates and cook them...

# Chapter Eight

# TRANSLATING YOUR NEEDS INTO ACTION

## *THE UNMENTIONABLE MALADY*

The word Homesickness is thoroughly old-fashioned. The thing itself is not.

Many transplants get an attack of the unmentionable malady about two or three months after settling into a new place where they're going to stay for a year or more. The change doesn't have to be intercontinental. Interstate within the same country is often enough. Some people cope extremely well, some suffer; a few go to pieces.

It doesn't only affect those who have changed their place of abode. A complete change of lifestyle will bring it on too. Human nature needs a period of adjustment to new circumstances. Even seedlings wilt a little after transplanting; then they push fresh roots into the fertile soil, and thrive!

Young lovers get married with bells and veils and weeping mothers. They rush off on a romantic honeymoon, determined to be Happy Ever After.

Then they get home and real life starts. How many couples can truthfully say that the third to the sixth months of their marriage were perfect bliss?

She wonders what happened to the adoration in his eyes.

He wonders why the resourceful little kitchen fairy of their courtship days explodes if she comes home half an hour after him and finds he hasn't put the dinner on.

He who once insisted on carrying the smallest parcel for her now expects that she help him change a car tyre.

The stubble stays on his face for half the weekend, until it's time to "go out with the boys".

His gallant, charming bachelor friends have turned into egoistic boors in three short months — all they want to do is take him to the pub.

He wants to know why she *must* always leave the petrol tank empty.

Both, secretly or openly, long for their carefree single days once in a while. But after another few months they learn to compromise. They discover the positive side to their new condition, and this is where the happy marriage starts.

## THE STAGES OF CULTURE SHOCK

The situation of a person settling down in a foreign environment is quite similar. The decision to move took some thought, inquiry and soul-searching, just like a decision to get married. Once it has been made, it has to be publicly announced, and defended against carpers and doomsayers.

The prospective migrant finds himself explaining his move to doubters. He enthusiastically praises the posting to Malaysia as a step up in his career. There's always a colleague or a relative who knows something negative about the country; Aunt Myrtle has this story about natives and rogue elephants, but — "don't be ridiculous there are no elephants in Malaysia; this is a promotion for me; the climate is idyllic, just the thing for Becky's asthma; Fanny will love to be waited on hand and foot by an army of white-coated servants; it's a problem-free country you never see on the network news; that ecology thing isn't in Malaysia, it's in Antarctica; of course they have motor cars, anyway the firm is sure to provide rickshaws!"

Fanny has read a couple of books and can tell her friends that she will live in a villa under swaying coconut palms surrounded by friendly natives in thatched huts, that most of the country is untouched jungle or rubber plantations, that the Malays are nature's own gentlemen, that without the need to do housework she will improve her piano playing, and that the yellow fever Mrs Jones has been gossiping about isn't in Malaysia at all, it's in Bengal.

Little Becky may have been promised a couple of pet monkeys by enthusiastic parents. She won't start to miss her grandma and her kindy friends until the family has left.

Getting the packing done, the house cleared, cats and dogs boarded out, affairs settled for two years keeps Jim and Fanny busy for the next few months. There is little time to think! After a few tears at parting, the little family boards a plane in a state of exhausted euphoria, ready to enjoy their stay in Malaysia to the full.

The first few weeks are a whirl of activity. Only Becky hangs on to mummy's skirts, cries and wheezes a lot more than she should, refuses to go to the new kindy and wants to be taken along everywhere. Jim and Fanny are invited to parties almost every night. As a senior officer in a respected firm he has to be introduced to other staff, to local business partners, government officials. "We were presented to the Sultan's third cousin at the club!" Fanny exults in her early letters home.

Fanny is eagerly grabbed by a number of women's circles and women's organizations. The house provided by the company is spacious and pleasant. Two servants are already here "but we are thinking of getting a second maid and a gardener" as she casually writes to an old school friend who used to have nicer toys and better clothes than Fanny did.

Letters home are irregular, gleeful and short; there's so much going on I hardly have time to write! We're feeling fine, the country is wonderful, wish you were here!

After four to six weeks, Jim begins to find that not quite everything is the way it should be. Coworkers have a way of agreeing to everything he says and then doing something different. The driver clocks up a lot more mileage than he logs with Jim aboard. But Jim is busy, while Fanny is not. She is hit hardest by the homesickness, or the culture shock, when it comes.

There is this constant heat, its effects magnified by moving into and out of air-conditioned houses and cars all day. Those insects weren't in Bengal after all, but right here in Kuala Lumpur. Becky is covered in red spots that itch and swell and the doctor only said they were "normal" and recommended baby ointment. The servants never understand what they are told; they smile secretly each time Fanny demonstrates the way she wants something done. The driver and the cook keep up a constant bickering; the gardener flirts shamelessly with the second maid and seems to spend more time on the kitchen verandah than among the flowerbeds. And he a married man, too!

That friendly Mrs Aminah who invited Fanny to tea tried to sell her rubies and got quite shirty when the offer was refused. Roaming packs of stray dogs howl at night. KL traffic would drive anyone crazy. TV programmes are hopeless. Decent magazines are a month old by the time they get here, and horribly expensive. Fanny gets whistled at when she goes to the shops and this horrid old woman actually patted Becky on the cheeks! It's impossible to find potatoes that will mash properly and we can hardly drink the milk.

This is when the postman is eagerly awaited every morning, when people ring up the Post Office in a rage which is aggravated if the person at the other end speaks Malay. A public holiday? How was I supposed to have known that? Jim is away on a business trip. No letters for me? Impossible! Why doesn't mother, sister, friend write? Here we are miserable and forsaken and Becky has asthma again — and our nearest and dearest simply ignore us and go on with their own lives!

Some families run up huge phone bills at this stage of their adjustment. It's so comforting to hear mother's voice. It's easy to chat on for 10 minutes; the small catch is that this costs 40 dollars! STD makes it easy for an intelligent child to ring up his cobbers back home, too, as Adrian Mole fans may remember. When the phone bill arrives, families have an earnest talk; if that doesn't work a small padlock is illegally affixed to the phone.

After four or five months, the family learns to cope with the new life. Becky has settled down in her kindy at last, Fanny is into sports and has found a competent piano teacher. The second amah has left. The Mrs Aminahs and royal third cousins of this world are relegated to their proper place in the scheme of things. Fanny has given up trying to referee each skirmish between the cook and the driver so the two belligerents have lost interest.

Life is taking on a normal rhythm. We live here now.

## *CUSHIONING THE SHOCK*

Culture shock can be cushioned. There is no foolproof method for doing this, but here are two essentials:

1) Don't compare.
2) Get out and about.

The quickest way to ruin any new relationship is to compare the present partner with the last one. This applies to employment situations too. The New Boss is a knight in shining armour during the "honeymoon period", then he becomes a grouchy, egocentric, predatory individual (qualifications vary) who finally evolves into an ordinary employer — unless he is constantly compared with that epitome of human perfection, the Last Boss.

This principle applies to New Countries.

Don't run down your own country in comparison with Malaysia during your first delirious weeks here, and don't run down Malaysia in comparison with your own when the real-life lag hits you. Not even in the privacy of your own thoughts. It's unwise, it's obviously illogical, it's unfair to both countries concerned. That won't worry the countries, but it will make your life very much harder.

## Be Positive

Find positive things in your new environment, practise just a little bit of self-deception if you need it. Mothers with small children do that anyway — hasn't Fanny told Becky that cod liver oil tastes delicious, that she'll love the scratchy wool sweater granny knitted for her, and that school is ever such fun? Tell yourself that the climate is mild, that the cosmopolitan mix of people in Malaysia's streets is exciting, that orchids in the garden borders are just so exotic.

In your own home environment, you lived among a "support group" though you never thought of them in these terms: close and distant family, workmates, friends, the shopkeepers and tradesmen you were in daily contact with, professionals and government officials whom you knew you could call on if there was a need.

Once you have built up this network in the new country, you have your own place in life again. Homesickness or culture shock stem fom the feeling, almost fear, of not belonging where you are, but where you were.

The prime support group, the extended family, is not with you; spouse and children are fellow-sufferers. There is one Instant

Family Replacement however: your Community Association.

## *Check Out Your Community Association*

There are American, British, French, Japanese, Italian, German Associations in Kuala Lumpur (and some in Penang); they may be contacted through a compatriot met at a cocktail party, or through one's Embassy or High Commission. For some newcomers they provide a chance to speak the mother tongue once in a while. Most of them have briefing notes for new arrivals, ranging from a couple of cyclostyled sheets to the efficient desktop publication of the German-speaking Women's Group. These groups help house-hunters. The younger members advise the parents of young children on preschool education. They often know a well-recommended servant who's looking for work. They meet for tea, coffee, sport.

## *Coping in the Outstation*

Expatriates who are living and working in small towns, "outstations" in Malaysian English, often take longer to settle down than their friends in KL or Penang. This is partly because life in up-country Malaysia looks rather primitive to a person used to other things; if it's any comfort, many city-bred Malaysians regard a posting to the jungle wilds as Simply The End. Some local women decline to shift, leaving the husband "outstation" to manage as best he can and come home for weekends and holidays. But expatriates seldom find a support group in such places until they have laboriously constructed one, a very small one, for themselves. A foreign wife initially has nobody to turn to, and nothing to do besides housework. There's no Italian Women's Association in Alor Star!

From your own group, you have to move out and meet others. This is important. Nobody is required to make dozens of bosom friends with whom to share the innermost secrets of their hearts, but it is important to know and interact with people. Fellow-expats, locals. At tennis you will meet players of all nationalities — but

167

how do you get introduced at a tennis club? Through friends, that's how.

## What's On?

You may find the political pages of the Malaysian newspapers puerile, but read them anyway so you know what the cocktail party chatter is about. "MM" doesn't stand for Mighty Mouse! Pay extra attention to the local pages. In Kuala Lumpur, the *Malay Mail* contains a lot of hometown news. Scan the film advertisements, the sports news; matches, games and fixtures are announced, in sports you've never heard of (*sepak takraw?* What's that?). Most of the films are in Malay, Chinese or Indian. What's offered in English may be third-rate cowboy or unmitigated blood and gore. But keep an eye open or you'll miss *Gone With the Wind* on its one-and-a-half-day season. The "blockbusters" usually get to KL within a month of their international release.

Public festivals and processions are announced in the news-papers if they involve road closures. This is useful knowledge unless you like to get caught in a traffic jam on the way to somewhere else. If it's a religious procession, go along, watch, take a camera. It'll be a colourful, noisy spectacle that will make excellent reading in letters home, and bring you nearer to the people of your host land.

## Clubs

Every Malaysian knows that Europeans Must Have a Club. It's de rigueur, just like the gin-tonics English women jolly well have to drink. Some expatriates have lived here for several years without one and still manage to live happy useful lives, but the great major-ity do join a club of some sort.

There are half a dozen clubs in Kuala Lumpur, from the prestigious Royal Selangor Club to more liberal and less expensive establishments. Membership is usually by introduction; some firms provide club memberships as part of the salary package, others expect their employees to pay their own.

The expatriate businessman will soon discover that the club and the golf course are places for informal meetings, discussions that may start something big but don't commit anybody as yet. The serious part of the negotiations will take place in the office on Monday morning, but many a huge deal grew from a seed sown on the fertile green of the Selangor Royal Golf Club. Bad news for poor golf players and non-golfers? Malaysia with its year-round outdoor sports climate may be a good place to take up the sport. Look at the bright side: no prospective business partner will seriously object to being the better player in a twosome...

It may be a good idea to ask parents of your children's schoolmates what clubs they belong to. Schools and clubs interact in many ways; in the afternoon school friends like to practise sports or play together at the club. In smaller towns, the club often has the only swimming pool; public pools are not very numerous even in KL, and they're usually very crowded. An expatriate family would get stared at, to put it mildly!

## Voluntary Work

There is much scope for volunteer work in Malaysia. Social services that are provided by government in other countries are run by charities here, and charities are notoriously hard-up. They can't afford to employ the skilled professionals they need. Physiotherapists, occupational therapists, speech therapists, specialist teachers are always in demand; the "expat wife" whose husband's contract forbids her to take on paid employment can make meaningful use of her professional qualifications and gain new experience.

"Lay persons" also help with charitable work, in the form of fund-raising or clerical assistance — and somebody has got to attend the fêtes and bazaars and buy all those raffle tickets, too. Many Malaysian charities would be in dire straits without the constant and generous support of foreign women.

## *Hobbies*

Sometimes a hobby leads to contacts. Many hobbies can be practised by one person all by himself or herself, but how much more
interesting, how much more fun (hobbies should be fun!) to share
with fellow-enthusiasts! Needlework in all its permutations, music,
collecting from A to Z — whatever your hobby, there is somebody
in Malaysia who shares it, and would like to compare notes. Tuition
in every conceivable subject is available in the bigger towns, music
up to the highest level, painting in inks, in oils, in batik, woodcarv-
ing. Every new arrival should take a basic Malay course, too,
another good way to meet people.

## *Sports*

Sport is written with a capital "S" in Malaysia. All the usual sports
are played here, non-professional clubs are eager for keen new
members. A few unusual sports are played here too: *sepak takraw*
("kick the cane ball"), competitive kite-flying with elaborate rules,
and top-spinning. The latter two aren't in the Olympic curriculum
yet, though *sepak takraw* is an official sport at the Asian Games.

Hashing, a peculiar predilection for crashing through the undergrowth at dusk shared by otherwise respectable folk, was actually
invented and perfected in Kuala Lumpur in the late 1930s. The
Mother Hash has kindled baby hashes on most continents. Some
Malaysian Hashes run mixed, others distinguish between Harriers
and Harriettes who run chastely on segregated evenings.

## *Music and Drama*

If stumbling along hedgerows with farm curs yapping at your heels
doesn't appeal, there are choirs in Kuala Lumpur and Penang,
classical and modern music ensembles, amateur dramatic groups.
The clubs are the usual venues for the performing arts, so are some
schools and associations. You've got to go out there and find out
what's going on — even without great histrionic talent, you could

be one of the crowd that cheers the coronation of Henry V.

## *Moving Along*

Old hands at frequent relocations advise the new arrival to join more activities than he intends to keep up. A keen chorister may find that the choir in Penang never sings his favourite music; after a few months he drops out again. Cricket, which he hadn't played since school, is thoroughly enjoyable with a crowd of good sporting fellows, and he's found this informal chess group, too. His wife went to every coffee morning and "playgroup" meeting she was invited to for the first two months, now she is finding her feet and chooses the crowd whose company she enjoys most, whose interests she really shares. By the fifth or sixth month an expatriate is usually acclimatized, ready to pull his or her weight and enjoy life to the full, ready to help other new arrivals settle in.

If none of the existing hobby groups cater for your specific needs, why not start a new one?

Found your own musical or artistic circle, with a constitution and rules and membership, or simply as an informal gathering as and when the mood strikes. Form a support group for handicapped people; volunteer to provide transport for inmates at an Old Folks Home, read aloud to the blind, give drawing lessons to children in the school for the deaf.

Offer to give tuition to people who need it — there is a constant demand for private English teachers here, some locals or expatriates want to learn French or Japanese. If you're qualified, why not teach, either as a hobby or as a means of earning a little pocket money?

## *CHILDREN*

Grown-ups can make a reasoned decision to adapt themselves to a new environment. Their children find this much harder. They may or may not have enjoyed the trip; they may find the new house of some fleeting interest but fairly soon the question comes: "When are we going home, mummy?"

It is difficult to explain to very young children why we're suddenly living in a different house, why Jimmy and his cat are no longer next door, and why we can't visit granny every other day. They are likely to cry a lot more than normal, and cling to mummy's skirts.

In the absence of a familiar environment, mummy and her skirts are all that is left of the real world. It is important that his favourite toys and "security blankets" are packed in such a way that they are accessible at once. A little boy who cries for his Kermit doesn't want it when the crates get here next month, he wants it now! This is not the time to tell him he shouldn't act like a baby. With the world as he knew it yanked away from under his feet, what else can he do but cower in a corner and cry for mummy (and Kermit)?

Spend a lot of time with young children. Attend to their needs, feed them, bathe them, put them to bed yourself, even if you have got a baby amah. Have her in the room with you; the child will learn to accept her, grudgingly at first but with trust as time proceeds. Mummy's presence in the weaning-over period is essential.

Small children, even their school-age brothers and sisters, may not want to play with strangers however enticingly introduced as "your new friends". A newcomer can upset a whole play group by his anti-social antics.

Diplomacy and tact are needed. Mother should invite one friend with a child about the same age to come and have tea with her. Tommy is on his home ground here; the visitor is the stranger. His mother's invitation to look after little Bobby who would like to play with him, worded as a suggestion not an order, may get things started. Plenty of toys must be available, none of them Tommy's favourites so he won't suddenly feel obliged to defend his property.

Some children love entering a new school or kindergarten, others hate it. Sometimes it is a good idea to send them for half an hour a day only, just before closing time when the other pupils are busy with their own activities and don't spend too much time scrutinizing and ragging the stranger.

Encourage grandparents and other relatives at home to send separate letters to those of the children who can read, communications which they may keep secret beyond a casual "Oh, mum, granny sends you her regards!" This establishes the child's autonomy, confirms him as a valid person in his own right, not just an appendix of a recently relocated family. Getting a stamped, sealed letter addressed to "Miss Jane Brixton" is a very different thing from casual "kisses to Mary, Jane and Billy" at the end of a letter addressed to the parents.

School-age youngsters may hit it off with a new class, or they may not. Most of them miss their friends at home. This was their support group, the "gang" they went on outings and shared secrets with.

Sometimes neither the parents nor the child settle into the new school well. The standard of education differs widely from one country to another. A new student's poor performance may be due to the fact that he has been put into a class not appropriate to his academic standard. Mother, unaware of this fact, blames him for laziness. This will make him feel even worse about the new school, and the change of abode in general.

Be very tactful when attempting to comfort a suddenly very grouchy 13-year-old! He does long for his friends, but he would consider it "sissy" to admit to such sentimental nonsense. He compensates by regarding all the kids at his new school, their mode of dressing, the teachers, the school buildings and the curriculum as "gross" or whatever the new word of disapprobation is.

The parents have to make an effort to overcome their own adjustment problems as fast as possible, or disregard them while considering the childrens'. Are John and Mary in the school and the class they should be in, academically and socially? Do they have the kind of clothes, use the kind of equipment the other students have?

Frugality is a virtue, but it can carry a penalty. "These shoes are prefectly good, you don't need others!" Maybe so as far as the quality of the shoes is concerned, but if your John wears the only polished shoes in a school full of sneakers he will be laughed at. Being "out of fashion" is an unforgiveable sin in the eyes of the peer group, the group John has to fit into, urgently, or be an unhappy loner. Would his mother wear a dressing gown and curlers to a Palace reception? Carrying a schoolbag when all the other kids use cane baskets is quite as ridiculous!

Encourage school-age children to write to their friends, send home photos (and keep an eye on the telephone!). They will have a great many secrets to communicate so don't ask too many questions. As they find new friends in the new country, the red-hot urgency will go out of the home correspondence; until then it is a lifeline.

Teenagers usually like the idea of travelling the world and visiting places. Some take to life in Malaysia like ducks to water. Others don't. A lot depends on their new school here, and how they manage to fit in. Some miss the freedom to drive their own cars (the legal driving age here is 18), others are puzzled by the restricted social life of young Malaysians. They fear to lose contact with the home country, their age-group and its culture. The Malaysian music and fad scene may be months behind the rest of the world; records, magazines and tapes are comparatively expensive.

Many young people like to keep in touch with their friends back home through the exchange of tape recordings. Besides conversations and peer group news, the latest in the way of music can be relayed in this way.

Parents should encourage this sort of "anchor" system up to a point. Like their elders, teenagers who cling entirely to the Good Old Country fail to acclimatize in the new.

Expatriates of all age groups must be aware that while most hallucinogenic drugs are available in Malaysia, their possession and use is strictly illegal. That goes from "pot", considered comparatively harmless by some users, to "hard drugs" like heroin and its derivatives. A person found in possession of 15 or more grammes of heroin or its equivalent is considered a trafficker, and the penalty for trafficking is death.

Malaysia does execute convicted drug traffickers regularly. Citizens or foreigners are equal before the law.

## EDUCATION

The medium of instruction in Government Schools is Bahasa Malaysia. The bulk of expatriates here send their children to private schools where they will be taught in English, German, French, Indonesian or Japanese.

These schools are expensive, and often have long waiting lists. Parents should inquire, and reserve places for their children, as soon as their postings to Malaysia are confirmed. Even the more exclusive kindergartens have waiting lists!

Many of the foreign-language schools only go up to year 6 or 7, the time when the child would enter secondary school in his home country. A number of foreign schools go up to year 13 or the baccalaureate; these are considered to be of excellent standard and are usually well patronized. But the courses offered may not suit the individual's requirements; the family must consider whether to enrol their child at school here, or in Singapore, or leave him in the home country. The decision to leave a child behind can be heartbreaking, and it is usually the mother who suffers most.

A few possible solutions are outlined here. These are only suggestions; they cannot take the decision off the family's shoulders.

1) Discuss the question with the child himself first.

It's his life, after all. At 14 or 15 he may not have an overwhelming interest in his future career; on the other hand he will resent being haggled over by all his relations and finally informed about his fate.

175

2) Has the child got any personal preference?

Is he attached to the family to such a degree that boarding school is out of the question? Has he a brother, a cousin, a good friend at boarding school whom he would be quite happy to join there?

3) Can the child be left with a relative?

Close relatives may be prepared to board a nephew so he can attend day school with his cousins. If he gets on well with them, and isn't made to feel the "poor relation", this can be an ideal solution. Avoid leaving a healthy 15-year-old with a septuagenarian granny, though!

4) Don't feature any solution as a punishment.

Don't make a domestic warfare issue out of your child's education! "Just wait till you get to boarding school — none of your nonsense there!" is as bad as "With manners / academic results / a hairstyle / like yours, I'd be ashamed to let the masters at St Xilian's see you!" or "He's such a lot of trouble I'd better handle him myself!"

5) Can you teach the child at home?

This is a solution for the studiously inclined who work well on their own and is more suitable for the short term. The education authorities of Australia, New Zealand and Canada have correspondence courses designed for the children of farmers in remote areas, but they are also excellent for home-teaching in foreign countries. Mother has to act in a supervisory capacity; this can be a stumbling block if strong personalities are involved. Some families hire a local tutor to work with the student; many a teenager takes a "real" teacher more seriously than his own mum.

## HEALTH IN THE TROPICS

With a few sensible precautions, Malaysia is a safe and healthy country to live in. Travellers' "shots" are no longer required in the region, malaria precautions are not necessary for anyone who stays in the populated areas. Public and private health facilities are of good standard.

Dr E.V. Haller, one of Germany's foremost specialists on tropical medicine, lists the most common causes of ill health in hot countries as follows:

Fevers, enteric infections, parasites, skin infections, venereal disease, poisonous bites and stings.

## *Fever*

Malaria does exist in Malaysia, but it is not common in towns. Expatriates whose work takes them to new land development areas, into the jungle or towards the Thai border should take prophylactics. They are available at any doctor's, pharmacist's or government dispensary. Like other preventatives, they must be taken regularly to be of any use, of course.

There is a certain amount of dengue haemorrhagic fever in poorly drained urban and suburban areas. The early symptoms are high fever, red spots, and the appearance of red or blue blotches on the skin if it has been even slightly pressed. If a person seems to be suffering from "measles" that last longer than they ordinarily should, consult a doctor.

The best protection against vector-borne diseases are mosquito screens on all windows of the house. The house compound must be kept clean, undergrowth and long grass regularly trimmed, possible breeding sites like empty bottles, tins, coconut shells, etc, eliminated. Stagnant water collects in such containers, and that's where mosquitoes breed.

It is actually illegal to breed mosquitoes in Malaysia. The municipal authorites are permitted to enter private premises to check for mosquito breeding places; if any are found the occupant is fined.

Chemical mosquito sprays, coils and repellants have their place in getting rid of the pests. It must be remembered that all three contain poisonous substances, and that their cumulative effect may affect human livers and kidneys.

Wearing long sleeves and long trousers or skirts out of doors is partial protection. This is especially true in the evening, when the mosquitoes "rise"; keep this in mind when choosing the clothes for a garden party or barbecue!

Small children should not be allowed to play naked in the garden. This exposes them to too much sun, insect bites, and public censure. Nudity in small *kampung* boys is acceptable but considered a sign of poverty. Servants and visitors alike would be embarrassed to see naked infants and toddlers disporting themselves on the floor of an expatriate's house.

A cold in the tropics acts and feels like a cold anywhere else. Maybe a little worse, because the patient feels hot from the fever and hot from the climate, and the doctor has just forbidden cold drinks, cold showers and air-conditioned rooms! Take aspirin and plenty of lukewarm liquid and don't waste your money on antibiotics. Like any other cold, it'll pass.

## Enteric Infections

In East Malaysia there is such a thing as nationalistic cholera. Any Malaysian who's returned from a visit to Brunei and gets stomachache, any Bruneian who's returned from a visit to Sarawak or Sabah and gets stomachache is immediately suspected of having picked up cholera "in those parts". We have no cholera in our own country, of course, but "those foreigners..."

The rare cholera outbreaks in Malaysia are well publicized to warn the travelling public away from the area for the duration. They are nearly always traced to contaminated water supplies, something residents in proper houses in the large towns don't have to worry about.

*Ulu* (upcountry) residents and travellers must boil all drinking water supplies, and take care not to swallow water while taking their bath in the river. It is better to use boiled water for toothbrushing, too.

The best immediate treatment for cholera, until medical help can be obtained, is to make the patient drink large quantities of luke-warm water with sugar and a pinch of salt in it, and keep him warm. People don't die of the diesease itself but of dehydration. The fruit water of a coconut (NOT the coconut "milk"!) is excellent for this purpose. Patent diarrhea medicines are useless to deal with cholera.

Urban housekeepers have no problems with drinking water supplies, but this does not give them a licence to be careless. Everybody must wash their hands after visiting the toilet and before eating. Fresh foods and vegetables must be washed carefully, kitchen refuse must be disposed of at once, in fly-proof containers. Shellfish and crustaceans are best avoided if there is any danger of enteric infections, they are notorious carriers. If there is a "cholera scare" on in your area, don't eat raw vegetables or unpeeled fruit. Surely you'd prefer a few days' shortage of Vitamin C to a few weeks of cholera?

## *Parasites*

Parasites are fairly common in the tropics; they can be controlled by proper food hygiene but they cannot be completely avoided. Your doctor or baby clinic nurse will advise you on the need to de-worm the whole family from time to time.

If one member has worms, it is a good idea to dose the whole family including the amahs. De-worm the pets while you're at it. Vermifuges come in various forms, syrups are available for small children.

Jungle travellers are warned against walking barefoot around villages, especially near the washing places which often serve as open-deposit latrine as well. This is the way to pick up hookworms, a parasite very much harder to get rid of than the comparatively common roundworm.

Expatriates who travel and work in up-country locations should have stool samples examined in a diagnostic lab from time to time,

179

and take appropriate action if they find themselves infested.

## Skin Infections

The most common skin troubles suffered by expatriates in the tropics are prickly heat, fungal infections and sunburn.

The first two are easily avoided by the use of porous, well ventilated clothes made of cotton or linen, and open sandals in preference to shoes. Take as many showers a day as you like, but don't use more than a touch of mild soap. Strong soaps can destroy skin bacteria and actually encourage some fungi.

Sunburn is avoided by the use of long-sleeved, long-legged garments and sun hats. Dont' lie on the beach baking in the sun — unless you want to be baked.

## Venereal Disease

VD is preventable; the careless must seek medical attention at once if they have contacted one of these infections. There are VD clinics in the major hospitals, but persons engaged in the vice trade are not obliged to attend for check-ups. Caveat emptor!

Prostitution is outside the law in Malaysia. Brothels are set up under respectable fronts like barber shops, massage parlours, model agencies and the like; bona fide hairdressers, models, waitresses suffer from the reflected ill fame.

Our northern neighbour is often quoted as the source of all sin and wickedness, and all the VD, in Malaysia. Prostitution is certainly a flourishing industry in some parts of Thailand; lecherous tourists are strongly advised to use proper protection. Some strains of the common kinds of VD are not responding to conventional treatment any more.

A number of AIDS cases have occurred in Malaysia.

## Bites and Stings

Insect bites may be painful, but unless the little buzzer carried some fever they are harmless. Most newcomers develop tolerance against common mosquito bites within a few weeks; until then, mosquito bites may become swollen and should be cleaned with disinfectant.

A very unpleasant insect often found in the gardens is the Painted Fly. It looks like a small moth with bright black and yellow bars across its wings. Its bite becomes infected, throws up a boil, subsides and comes up a second time a few weeks later! It is advisable to spray under bushes and along lawns to control this diurnal pest, and keep an eye on small children playing in the garden.

Scorpion and centipede stings should be seen by a doctor. They are not fatal except for babies, but they can become painfully inflamed and turn blue. Proper medical treatment prevents prolonged suffering.

It is very seldom that snakes are met in urban areas. If anyone is bitten by a snake, don't waste time scrutinizing its markings and ascertaining the shape of its eyeballs — rush the patient to the nearest clinic. Give the doctor a rough description of the reptile and the location, he'll know which anti-serum to use. Family members can be sent on a search-and-identify mission, but get the patient to hospital first.

Snakes are caught by pinning them down behind the head with a forked stick. This sounds simple; it isn't. If a snake is in the house, try to chase it out. Making noise by banging pots and pans, etc, will get on most reptiles' nerves; leave the escape route visibly open to let it slither outside.

Snakes don't attack unless they are cornered. A zealous watchdog that takes on a cobra may be bitten, or have poison spat in its eyes. Rush your pet to the vet if this happens. Few dogs survive a snake bite. If they've been splashed they need their eyes washed clean of venom at once to save their sight.

One word of warning if a cobra has been killed in or near a house: cobras come in pairs. Stand by for an angry mate a few days after the first killing!

181

The few snakes that turn up always seem to do so when only women are at home. Luckily, agonized screams of *"Ular! ular!"* (Snake!) alerts any man within hearing distance; it is quite in order to ask your driver, gardener, even a Council worker busy down the road, to come and deal with the intruder.

## MEDICAL FACILITIES AND HEALTH CARE

Government and private hospitals in Malaysia are of good standard; for specialist treatment many Malaysians and expatriates go to Singapore where there are a Japanese and an American hospital too.

Most Malaysian babies are born at the local maternity hospital. Private clinics also offer obstetric care. Many expatriate women decide to have their babies here, others prefer to go off on long furlough and give birth in their own home countries.

A nation-wide network of Mother and Child Health Clinics caters for the needs of the coming generation. Antenatal care is obtained at these centres, the usual childhood vaccinations are administered free. Private doctors and clinics also provide these, and general infant and pediatric care, for appropriate fees.

The best health care is, of course, not to get sick in the first place! A sensible diet and regular exercise do much towards pre-serving health in the tropics as well as anywhere else. Exercise classes offer yoga, aerobics, dance; sport and athletics cater for the more energetic.

The new arrival should beware of exercising too strenuously until he is acclimatized. No Malaysian jogs under the midday sun ("Mad dogs and Englishmen...")?), even farmers take a couple of hours off at noon. They're not lazy, they're sensible. The time to exercise is in the cool of early morning, from half past six till eight, or after four in the afternoon. After a vigorous session, take a long drink of cold water to replace lost liquid. It isn't the sun that gives people "sun stroke"; the modern name for that complaint is "heat exhaustion" and it's caused by dehydration.

## *OUT AND ABOUT*

Picnics fall somewhere between an outing and a sport. Locals stare in disbelief at families unpacking their sandwich hampers on the lawn in public parks; the socially acceptable picnic sites are waterfalls, rapids, officially recognized beauty spots in national parks. We work for our pleasure by lugging those hampers along jungle paths, or at least driving up rough roads into the carefully kept jungle of a public picnic site.

More extended than a picnic are seaside holidays in chalets, rented out at very reasonable rates on the lesser known beaches. Now at last you can live in a leaf-thatched cottage under swaying coconut trees. Just keep clear of those trees during a high wind. A ripe coconut weighs up to 1.5 kg, and it's hard!

If all the family's members are of walking age, a lot of fun can be had hiking and trekking in Malaysia's National Parks.

## *Planning Your Trips*

Visit Malaysia Year is over, but Malaysia is worth visiting any time at all. Foreign residents want to go home for some of their vacations, of course. But, having come this far already, why not spend at least some local holidays in the country? Expatriates from Australia and New Zealand should remember that the southern winter roughly coincides with Malaysia's "summer", the dry season. When Sydney is all gloom and drizzle and Wellington a howling gale, Malaysia's beaches glow in the warm sunshine of everlasting summer.

Malaysia is a good staging point for regional holidays. Find a resourceful travel agent and see what she can come up with: some package holidays within Malaysia, especially if the trip involves crossing the South China Sea, are actually cheaper if they are booked from Singapore, and by foreign passport-holders! Luxurious beach hotels in Sarawak and Sabah offer family "packages" that are hard to refuse. Fancy a weekend of swimming and snorkelling and windsurfing interspersed with wining and dining and doing blissfully nothing? This is one of the situations where a foreign passport is an advantage. Make full use of it!

Sumatra is just a hop across Malacca Straits; Lake Toba is a popular destination there. Thailand, particularly the beach resorts of South Thailand, is within reach of road, rail or air travel. Malaysians can drive their own cars up there, or rent campervans.

Singapore ranks as a shopping destination more than a holiday resort, but many Malaysians go there to attend concert and ballet performances.

Bali, that travellers' magnet, is a lot closer to Kuala Lumpur than to London — why not make the most of it now you're here?

Local holidays are the best of all. As there is a good road network over West Malaysia, one way to travel is by car. Get a good supply of maps and learn to read them. The friendly local chap you ask for directions may not understand exactly what it is you want to know, but he'd be far too polite to disagree with you!

If you are really lost, find a police station and ask for directions there. Your friendly rural cop may or may not speak much English, but he'll make an effort to understand your Malay. In a real emergency, find a phone and ring the nearst branch of the TDC. It is their duty to help you find your way.

The Malaysian Tourism Promotion Board (MTPB) publishes lists of the hostelries in the country, with indications about the standard. Hot and cold water in all rooms, air-conditioning, restaurants and other facilities are listed, as are the prices. Get a copy of this list, which is updated every year, before setting out.

The most basic accommodation in Malaysia is the "Chinese Hotel", often upstairs above a shophouse. A few rooms have been constructed with plywood partitions; each has two beds, mosquito-screened windows, a ceiling fan. Air-conditioning, if available, is an extra, the shared toilet arrangements are down the end of the passage.

From this very basic accommodation, standards range up to the international-standard hotel with every luxury and extravagance including the tariffs. In country towns, a three-story hotel with air-conditioned bedrooms, attached bathrooms and a coffee house downstairs is the norm; provided they are clean these places can be very pleasant. A lot depends on the management. One family of expatriate motor-tourists has spent their vacations in a small town in rural Kelantan for three years running, to be greeted on each return like long-lost relatives by the owner and his family.

Some visitors are disappointed with the way the more popular tourist spots look, especially after a public holiday. Big signs in many languages exhort the public to be careful and keep the place clean — so how did all this rubbish get here?

People dropped it, sad to say. The unfortunate turtles labouring up the East Coast beaches to lay their eggs are almost drowned in rubbish in some locations. Wildlife authorities report deaths of animals due to the ingestion of plastic bags.

In some places, park authorities patrol the picnic sites and actually slap fines on offenders; in most areas the park staff spend the

Monday After clearing away tins and plastic bags bobbing and swirling in the waters extolled as "crystal-clear" in the tourist pamphlets!

It is now possible to rent campervans in Malaysia though properly equipped and organized campsites are still scarce. As this mode of transport becomes popular, more motorcamps are coming up near the nation's most beautiful locations. A campervan saves hotel fees, eliminates cockroaches and noisy fellow guests (except the ones you brought along yourself) and permits the traveller to stay exactly where he likes. West Malaysia has good roads, too.

Another mode of travelling is by train. There are two main northsouth routes and one eastwest one; it is possible to take the train to Singapore and to Bangkok. Malayan Railways offer special railpasses for tourists who intend to cover a lot of ground. Find out about these from your travel agent. She can possibly wangle you extra privileges because you travel on foreign passports.

Many Malaysians travel by long-distance bus. Buses serve to a lot more destinations than the train does, and they are reasonably priced. During holiday seasons (Hari Raya, Chinese New Year, school vacations), it is not advisable to travel by train or by bus because every vehicle will be full to bursting point.

Bus journeys start from the main bus stations in town. Expatriate bus travellers should beware of a specialist beggar who haunts these places: usually a woman, she approaches passers-by with a sad story of how her handbag was stolen and she can't get home. Could you please give her M$ 46 or some such sum to buy a ticket back to Malacca? If necessary, she offers half a dozen starving children and an invalid elderly parent as a sure-fire inducement. When turned down, she may start to weep, or turn loudly abusive. It is best not to stand still to listen to her tale at all!

Young women travelling in buses should sit with other women if at all possible. Some men find the presence of a foreign female next to them on a bus seat too inviting, particularly so if she wears

*Malaysia's many offshore island resorts is a haven for those who love the outdoors and the sea.*

shorts! The solution to this problem, and a few others, is to travel in groups. The solo female bus traveller may be exposed to quite unpleasant hassling.

A number of ships sail around Malaysia's coast; those that take passengers are usually the ones that ply between the mainland and islands. There used to be a marine ferry service between East and West Malaysia, designed to encourage motor tourists from one side to visit the other, but it has been discontinued. Few people take a car with them when they cross the South China Sea unless they are going there for a long-term posting. Holiday visitors to East Malaysia can rent cars there if they like, though they won't get very far out of the coastal towns unless they get four-wheel drive vehicles. East Malaysian roads are not, tactfully expressed,

187

up to West Malaysian standards, though they're improving.

This should not put people off visiting the rugged part of the country. Malaysia's highest mountain is in Sabah, 4101-metre Mount Kinabalu. Malaysia's longest river, the Rejang, is in Sarawak, so are the country's biggest caves, Mulu.

The usual way to travel between East and West Malaysia is by air. There are regular flights between the main centres of both halves of the country; domestic flights connect the centres to the "outstations" in both East and West. The adventurous East Malaysia traveller shouldn't miss a chance to wing his way into the interior in a plane slightly bigger than a suburban bus, the Twin Otter.

One way of travel is not common in Malaysia: hitchhiking. Some motorists don't even know what a fellow means if he walks along the road and tips his thumb at every passing car!

Female hitchhikers, especially if they are young, are in danger of being thoroughly misunderstood. Nice Malaysian girls don't walk along the road and wait for strangers to pick them up. If (foreign) girls are walking along the road waiting for strangers to pick them up, they are obviously not nice girls...

## BIRTHS, MARRIAGES AND DEATHS

The doctor or midwife delivering a baby in Malaysia fills in the Birth Information slip and hands it to the parents. This piece of paper is essential for registering the child's birth, and getting a Birth Certificate.

The babies of expatriates must be registered at their parents' Embassies, High Commissions or Consulates. A child born here does not automatically qualify for Malaysian citizenship unless its parents are Malaysians.

Couples intending to marry have the choice between a religious ceremony or civil registration. Approved priests and religious officials are in fact Registrars; every marriage in Malaysia must be registered to be valid.

Expatriates who get married here often have their union solemnized by their Ambassador, High Commissioner or Consul, according to the laws of their own country. There may be legal formalities if people of different nationalities decide to marry; allow sufficient time for paperwork and complicatons between the first official application and Naming the Day.

In the unlikely event of an expatriate dying while in Malaysia, his consular officials must be notified at once. Bodies can be stored at the hospital morgue for a limited time; family members or friends have to make funeral or transport arrangements as soon as the legal formalities have been cleared.

There are Christian cemeteries of most denominations in Malaysia; they are usually prepared to grant a resting place to a deceased member of a group that is not represented here.

Tombstones of every variety can be ordered at the local stonemasons', who will produce monuments to specific designs. Such designs should be produced in the form of detailed drawings with very clear lettering on them. Many of the craftsmen are Chinese-educated; they may misunderstand oral directions and misspell inscriptions.

It is expensive and difficult to have a body embalmed and flown to the home country, but it is possible. Consult the local hospital for details and be sure to complete all the necesary paperwork at least several days before the proposed departure date.

There are crematoria in the larger Malaysian towns. It is sometimes more convenient to have a body cremated and the ashes brought to their final resting place overseas.

According to an expert, the most common causes of expatriate deaths in the tropics are traffic and flying accidents.

*—Chapter Nine—*

# HOW THE OTHER HALF LIVES

## *OUTSTATION AND THE GRASS ROOTS EXPAT*

The "typical expatriate", if there be such a thing, lives in a modest to splendid house in Kuala Lumpur or Penang and works for a big business company or on contract to the Malaysian government.

There are others. Some are working outstation, others *ulu*. Where's that?

"Outstation" is the rest of the country seen from one of the centres. The word is a colonial leftover, when people dreaded postings to malaria stations, or packed their womenfolk off to hill stations for the hot seasons. "Outstations" are widely regarded as "no place for women" by Malaysians! If a Malaysian government servant is transferred outstation, he often leaves his family in town while he roughs it in the jungle wilds of Betong or Grik or Sik.

Some banks charge a small clearing fee if presented with an "outstation" cheque; the telephone office distinguishes between a local call and an outstation call. In these cases, "outstation" simply means "long-distance". In Kota Kinabalu, a KL cheque is an "outstation cheque"!

"Ulu" is where you can't get to in a sedan car. Literally meaning "upriver", the term describes the headwaters of Malaysia's major rivers, mountainous regions difficult of access. The seasoned "ulu" traveller distinguishes between the areas which can be reached by four-wheel drive, those accessible by boat, and the others which require good boots and stamina.

Expats are found in both "outstation" and "ulu" places. Foreign teachers, often volunteers, may get an outstation posting at a large rural boarding school. Foreign doctors can be met with in small district hospitals, especially if they are engaged in research. Technical experts in the fields of agriculture, forestry, geology and similar disciplines obviously won't be delving or pruning or drilling on Merdeka Square in KL.

Graduate students from other Asian or overseas universities may be engaged in postgraduate work in Malaysia. Many of them spend at least some of their time outstation or *ulu*.

Outstation life is small-town life par excellence. Everybody knows everybody else and everybody else's business. The local dignitary's progress down the main street is noted with a polite nod by all the shopkeepers he passes; his cuppa is ready to his particular liking at the coffee shop, the news vendor saved him one copy of his favourite newspaper. Schoolboys inclined to pranks risk being recognized by any passer-by — "Eh, you're Pak Ahmad's lad, aren't you?"

There are many compensations to small-town life that make up for the absence of a well-stocked supermarket. House rents and servants' wages are lower than in town; foodstuffs, on the other hand, can be more expensive. Neighbours do mind each others' business, which cuts down on thefts and burglaries. A young woman walking home after dark won't be attacked, she'll be talked about. Everybody within earshot drops everything and comes running at a call of "Api! Ular!" or "Hantu!" (Fire, snake or ghosts).

In this cosy atmosphere, a newcomer sticks out like a sore thumb. A Japanese, Korean or other Asian should blend in by reason of his hair colour and general features. Not in a small town he don't! not even if he's a "foreigner" from Johor trying to speak Malay in Kelantan.

A Japanese agriculturalist working in a New Village (A Chinese security settlement established during the Emergency) in semi-rural Malaysia was puzzled and hurt at the way some elderly folks abruptly turned away when he appeared on the shop verandahs or in a village street, and refused to answer his greeting if he met them. His interpreter, after much pressing, finally told him that these were people old enough to remember World War II and considered all Japanese as "bad".

And then there's this East Malaysian native, a Christian to boot, who was refused his favourite pork-bone soup in a Chinese coffee shop somewhere in rural Kelantan. "Serving pork to Muslims is an offense!" the shopkeeper admonished the hungry traveller, "I'll get into trouble as much as you will!" — "But I'm a Kadazan, from Sabah!" — "Eh? What's that? What's your name anyway?" — "Jamil." —"Hah! I knew you were Muslim!" and the only dish on the menu that day turned out to be salt fish with bean sprouts.

A European female wearing knee-length skirts and no head-covering can meet an outraged reaction in a very remote, tradition-bound Malay village, especially during the fasting month. Luckily it is only a small proportion of the population that will prejudge a newcomer; sometimes the initial critics become friends or even grudging admirers. A lot depends on how the outsider behaves!

## ACCOMMODATION

Finding accommodation in an outstation may present some difficulties. There are no flats. One worker or researcher may not want to rent a whole terrace house. Boarding with a local family is a possibility, if any local family wants an expat boarder. Houses are usually full, and people don't want to give all the neighbours something to talk about.

Many expatriates in this situation find board, or share-rent a house, with colleagues. Some, especially researchers, stay with a Malaysian family a few days or weeks only. In either case, a few efforts to fit in with your host family's lifestyle will make for a pleasant, productive outstation or *ulu* period.

### Staying with a Malaysian Family Short-Term

You are already familiar with food taboos, and wouldn't dream of bringing a package of ham sandwiches into a Malay house or a bunch of sizzling beef *sate* into an Indian one.

Depending on the size of the house, you may be assigned a room to yourself, or billeted with a family member. Women visitors are more likely to be asked to share than men; putting her in a room with the daughter of the house shields her reputation, for which the host family is responsible for the duration.

Please consider this before grouching or laughing at the round-the-clock protection the family give you. Your ideas of privacy are radically different from theirs: they consider it unfriendly as well as morally unsafe to leave a good-looking young woman unescorted at any time. Inform them if you are going out, be it for a stroll in the bazaar, be it on a full-day field trip. If anything happened, if the neighbours found occasion for disparaging comment, the shame (which the object may be blissfully unaware of!) would reflect on the family.

193

Malaysians have ideas on privacy too. These are violated by a young person relaxing at home in overly-light attire, by washing being done other than in strict privacy, by — horrors! — undergarments being hung on the line. Take sufficient supplies of knickers for a short family visit; even panty hose fluttering in the breeze upsets some conservative souls. If you're staying for a month, standards will have to be relaxed. Find out where the women of the household dry their unmentionables.

This applies to menstruation. A short-term guest is strongly advised to pack used tampons or pads in a plastic bag and hide them in the bottom of her suitcase until she can discard them decently. A boarder has to take mama into her confidence about the disposal of yet another batch of unmentionables!

In an *ulu* setting, you have to learn how to take your bath in full view of the public, at an open well or by the riverside. This requires a pair of *sarung*. Dressed in one tucked around yourself under the armpits, bring up a bucket of water and start to soap your face, arms and lower legs. Then step knee-deep into the river and discreetly complete soaping under the *sarung,* never lifting it more than knee-high. Now you may swim a few strokes (careful of the *sarung* knot!) or pour water over yourself. Stand on the jetty for a minute to drip-dry, towel the exposed parts of the body, then pull the dry *sarung* over your head. As it falls down to cover you, untie the wet one and let it drop to the floor. One good method is to hold on to the dry cloth with your teeth! Once wrapped in the dry *sarung,* many women quickly wash the wet one. Go back into the house to complete dressing.

Men follow the same routine with a *sarung* or towel, tucked around the waist only. It is considered very offensive for a man to take off all his clothes. Little boys can run around naked; grown men don't skinny-dip even in all-male company. Before going deep into any river, ask the locals about the crocodile situation.

Older houses may have bathrooms with a shower only, or with a tap and a *tanki,* a cement water basin in which water is stored.

This is not a bathtub! Use the plastic dipper provided to pour water over yourself after soaping.

It is a good idea to bring along a few sheets of paper tissue if you are used to toilet paper; there may or may not be any provided. Many local people clean themselves with water; the left hand is employed for this task, and that's the reason why it may never, never be used to pass or handle food.

The toilet may be of the squat-type; sometimes toilet and bath facilities are in the same room. As a protection against parasite infestation, wear rubber sandals while using the toilet or having a shower. If the bathroom tap is the only place where clothes can be washed, one person's lengthy bathing and beautification operations will inconvenience the whole household. Get in there, lather up, sluice down, dry off and get out!

Be glad you have a door between yourself and mankind even if the bathroom is a bit primitive. In a real *ulu* setting, the bathroom may be the river, the toilet behind a discreet bush.

Do not streak from bedroom to bathroom in underclothes. A dressing gown should be worn, or the wonderfully versatile *sarung*.

## *"Just Treat Me Like One of the Family!"*

If you stay for a long time, Malaysians will eventually do that. Any family would. On a short-term visit, on the other hand, you have to be careful how you offer to help with housework even. The housewife may take it as a hint that her house isn't clean enough, her cooking not up to scratch. Baby-minding is one way a guest can usefully occupy his or her time. This leaves mama more time for chores, and the visitor can always plead an abiding love for little ones while he coaches a toddler in "Pussycat Pussycat Where Have You Been". Making your own bed early in the morning will prevent the housewife from having to do that, too.

One way to be admitted to kitchen duty is to express a strong desire to learn how to cook those delicious dishes. Women guests may succeed where men guests don't; a man's interest in the kitchen is misrepresented as interest in the girls of the household, who usually cluster there, especially if there are guests in the house.

Should house guests bring presents? This depends very much on the terms on which they are invited.

If a workmate asked you to come home to the *kampung* with him for Hari Raya, take along prettily wrapped toys for younger children (ask him for family details), something decorative like fancy dishes for his mother, scent or cologne for papa, a T-shirt from your own country, special foodstuffs. A few kilos of grapes are esteemed as a luxury in an outstation household far from the nearest supermarket; a sack of rice or half a dozen chickens looks like charitable contributions — "here's some food for you poor half-starved villagers!"

If you stay for more than a week, go along on the housewife's shopping expeditions and insist (nicely!) that you want to pay the bill. Be careful of offering presents of money straightout. This will be resented by some families. It is all right to give the children a few dollars when you take them for an outing to the local bazaar, or upon departure, but be very tactful or the gesture will look patronizing. Sometime a little joke helps matters along.

If you stay for more than just a couple of days, invite the family for a meal in the local restaurant or bazaar once in a while. This gives mama a spell from cooking, and it's your "treat" to say Thank You.

None of the above applies if you stay with a very wealthy family. For one thing their manners and style of living are very westernized — but it is still a nice touch to bring a present of some sort. What can you give the man who has a Mercedes, a Volvo and a BMW in his front porch? A printed tablecloth with New Zealand flowers and birds, a pair of Dutch clogs, a real Meissen ashtray. A souvenir-gift from your own country is always appreciated, and it doesn't carry "value" the way a gold-and-onyx paperweight would.

In a middle-class family, it is in order for a guest to tip the servant(s) on departure. Do this discreetly by visiting the kitchen, thanking Ah Moy for all the lovely meals she's cooked, apologizing for the extra trouble you've given her, and here's a little something ... The amount should be from $20 to 40; a few dollars would put her in the "child" category!

## *The Boarder*

As a boarder, you are renting one room in a private home. You may be taking your meals with the family, eat in the bazaar, or cook for yourself in the kitchen. Be sure these points are quite clearly understood when you make the rent agreement. Many families resent a stranger roaming aimlessly around the house, suspecting that he's snooping into their private affairs. Many an expatriate boarder is embarrassed to see the family immediately withdraw if he wants to sit on the porch, in the front room, in the garden, anywhere at all except in his own room.

Although you are a paying guest, you are still a guest of sorts. Both you and the family can stay on "good behaviour" for a couple of weeks, then you'll have to relapse to acting natural. But the above notes on dress and acceptable behaviour apply to a boarder as well as a visitor.

Adapt yourself to the family's lifestyle as much as is necessary to preserve harmony. Different ideas on noise levels can sometimes lead to disagreements. Do they play radios and TV loudly all night, or do you, and does either party object? Tell them politely that you need your sleep and would be grateful if they turned the volume down after 10 p.m. They may be too polite to tell you that some of your habits bother them, so keep your eyes and ears open for signals.

Do not fill the house with your friends or coworkers until you have ascertained that your host family doesn't mind. If they are Muslim and pray regularly, don't invite people at the prayers hours.

If you have invited friends, your hostess will feel obliged to serve them with a drink. Depending on how frequently you entertain, buy an extra bottle of cordial, an extra packet of tea from time to time as your contribution to the household stock. If you invite people for meals, be clear about the catering: a) you cook food which you bought specially for the occasion, b) you order food in from the local cook-shop, c) you pay your hostess extra to cook for your friends. Do not make her feel that you impose on her. Be discreet in your drinking habits. Neighbours may talk if your Muslim host family's rubbish bin is full of beer cans...

The simplest way is probably to take friends down to the bazaar for a *makan*. For one thing, you can drink what you like there!

Ask friends into your room after you have sat with the host family for five minutes. Do NOT invite friends of the opposite sex into your room, ever, except in quite a large group. Even then, conservative villagers will consider such proceedings "fast". Nobody will say much to you, but your hostess will be criticized, pitied, or suspected of complicity in bottomless decadence by half the village!

## *Rent-a-House*

Expatriates who are going to live outstation for a half a year or more may rent a terrace or *kampung* house in the township. Married couples usually do this, as do teams working together.

There is little choice of housing in smaller outstation towns; the local broker considers a bunch of ignorant foreigners a gift from heaven and charges you a rent commensurate with the very high status he respectfully estimates you at. If possible, make use of local contacts to reserve accommodation before your arrival; the rent can't very well be adjusted to the length of the tenants' noses if it has been fixed beforehand!

I am not aware that there are more insects outstation than in town, but they have less people to feed off so each of us gets more bites. If your house isn't air-conditioned, check that all the windows are mosquito-screened, and that the screens are in good order. In a real jungle location, learn how to protect your pressure lamps from the huge moths that flit in, suicide bent, soon after you have lit up after dusk. Sometimes the only safe place is in the privacy of a carefully closed mosquito net, even for reading or writing.

Ensure that the plumbing and kitchen equipment is in good order before taking a house. There may only be a gas ring in the kitchen; see if you can talk the landlord into putting in a proper stove. You may like to use an oven from time to time.

## *Outstation Shopping and Housekeeping*

Shopping outstation is a problem. There are wet markets and gro-cers' shops in most country towns and even the larger villages, but in the *kampung* each farmer grows his own vegetables, catches his own fish and rears his own chickens or goats. Learn to keep system-atic shopping lists: one for the nearest grocer, one for the wet market two villages away, one for the supermarket in the nearest township, one for visits to a big town when you can stock up on imported foods and cleaning materials.

It is possible to buy rice in any *kampung* shop in Malaysia. Bread is available practically everywhere, though it may be half a day old before it gets there. Butter is a different problem. Tinned butter and margarine are available in most places; if the stuff has been on the shelves for a while I'd prefer marge! Some jams are usually sold, as is *kaya,* a confection of coconut cream, eggs and sugar produced on the principle of lemon curd. Many outstation housewives make their own jam (pineapple is an easy-to-get favour-ite). Just limit each batch to three or four glasses, as preserves become mouldy very fast.

If there is electricity in your quarters, get a good fridge with an adequate-sized freezer. This makes planning and catering a lot easier.

If there is no electricity, learn how to use kerosene or spirit pressure lamps, to trim the wicks of a kerosene fridge, to cook with bottled gas or wood. If you live literally off the beaten track, in a river-based location, knowing how to drive and repair an outboard engine is a useful skill. Your company probably provides drivers with the boats, but in an emergency each member of the team should know how to drive a boat, or even how to paddle one if the engine is irretrievably broken down. On *ulu* or jungle projects, "Boy Scout Skills" come in useful, and so does a healthy sense of humour.

Many expatriates find it hard to live without a newspaper beside their breakfast plate. This is usually a problem of transport; how far are you from the nearest rail line or overland bus route? The local rag may be available by mid-morning, the KL papers by late afternoon. For news, you can always watch TV and listen to the radio; several foreign networks beam news programmes over Southeast Asia on shortwave.

## "INDECENT" BEHAVIOUR/DRESSING

Expatriates living outstation in their own quarters can live their own lives up to a point. They will be observed and commented upon. People who can't stand that shouldn't accept small-town postings, not anywhere on earth!

Two items most of us consider "my own business" are seen as public interest issues in small-town Malaysia: dress and personal morals.

To quote a Canadian Chinese woman who taught in several parts of Malaysia: "The smaller the town the bigger the dresses!"

Short skirts or miniskirts, tight spaghetti-strap dresses, high high heels and fish-net stockings are acceptable in KL or Penang. Not wildly popular in every segment of society, but acceptable. They are NOT ACCEPTABLE in a small Malaysian town or village.

A Muslim woman is expected to cover her arms, legs and head; a non-Muslim should have at least short sleeves, knee-length skirts, shallow necklines or collars. From a practical point of view, long sleeves and trousers are more comfortable in the heat of the sun. Conservative parents are upset if the teacher they entrust their children to turns up in "immoral" outfits.

There is no window to look into a man's soul, so how can the population of Kpg Ulu Ayer decide whether the new Malaria Eradication Officer is moral or not?

If she is female, she must not live alone. Boarding with a family is all right; if she rents quarters she should share them with another female. In the big towns there are "mixed flats" of young working people, but don't try that in Ulu Ayer! The foreign woman there must not be seen talking to one man alone, walking along the road with him at dusk or after dark, going for unchaperoned drives.

Some of these restrictions are impractical for an expatriate working woman, but often a bow in the direction of tradition can soothe local feelings. In schools, two or three female teachers usually share one set of living quarters; for the solo expat a live-in servant counts as a chaperone.

A woman can flout all or any of these restrictions, but she'll find herself attended, not to say pestered, by an unwanted gaggle of admirers. A woman living alone is seen as an invitation to all comers. Be a reckless free spirit by all means, but be sure you can cope with the consequences.

Some foreign researchers who had to work "outstation" for lengthy periods have found it convenient to wear wedding rings as part of their protective clothing.

Male expats don't get off scot-free either. Traditional law decrees that if a couple are inside a room unchaperoned, they have committed the misdemeanour of "close proximity" and are now considered engaged, with the girl's family pressing for speedy nuptials!

This law applies to Muslims only, but in a conservative *kampung* a foreign male teacher who detains one female student after class, for instance, could find himself in big trouble. Nobody, not even his headmaster, will believe that he was helping her with her trigonometry problems. The girl didn't necessarily give false testimony against him either, she may not even have been questioned. If she is alone together with a man, she is immediately accused of gross misdemeanour by every female within earshot. The closed door is considered as proof of wicked intent. Whether or not anything illicit took place is almost irrelevant.

A man accused of molesting a girl under these circumstances may claim trial and get off, but her reputation is compromised. Who'd want to marry her now?

If there is good and sufficient reason why a student has to be kept in after class, the teacher must ask another two or three persons of both sexes to be present — the cleaning lady or boarding house matron will do. It is better not to detain students in the classroom but in the school office, where the clerks and other teachers act as unwitting chaperones.

## THE IVORY TOWER

Indonesian students at Malaysian universities, most of whom are Muslims too, are not immune to culture shock. They stare in disbelief at the deeply veiled forms that glide past them in the corridors of learning, at radical students who break up a musical performance on campus because it happens not to be in line with their religious beliefs and tastes. They are amazed at the fact that in this country fast-breakers are not dealt with by the local religious authorities, but arrested by the Police!

Not all of the few European students at local universites fit in happily; the most quoted difficulties are the the high importance accorded to religion in Malaysia, and the "small-town mentality" of their fellow students.

It should be recalled that European universities started as centres of religious learning too; in some such institutions lecturers had to be clergymen until the last century. Some of Europe's and America's most famous universities are endowed and still run by churches.

Sometimes religion is misapplied to handle a personal misunderstanding. A foreign girl shared a hostel room with a local colleague who never removed her head coverings. All right, no problem...but it was! The Malaysian girl asked the hostel supervisor to allocate her a different room because she could never comb her hair properly, being unable to uncover it in the presence of a non-Muslim.

Obviously, these two young women didn't get on with each other from the start. Was the local girl forced to share the room

203

against her wishes? I would suspect so; the foreign student finished her year of Malay Studies with great academic success but with an unfortunate impression of Malaysians in general. She saw the episode as one of personal rejection.

The charge of small-town mentality is difficult to define and difficult to defend. Visiting academics never fail to praise the good manners of Malaysian students. "They're not as extroverted as our kids at home!" is one way of saying they're not too noisy — and at least one American lecturer has been heard to mutter that he wishes they did make a bit of noise from time to time, noise of the right kind!

Many Malaysian students are from small-town and rural backgrounds; despite intellectual curiosity and strong feelings they keep themselves reined in. This is how they were brought up.

Yes there are student demonstrations in Malaysia, but they're rare and, by international standards, almost decorous!

—*Chapter Ten*—

# "I WORK HERE!"

When it comes to business premises, facilities, equipment and staff, Malaysia has it all — in the towns. Up-to-date buildings rise in KL, Penang and Johor. The latest in the field of electronics and office machines is available here; the big business houses are on-line with East Malaysia, Singapore and the rest of the world.

Some foreigners who come to work in the tropics are amazed to learn that they will need suits and warm clothing. Office buildings, almost without exception, are air-conditioned, so are meeting halls, convention centres, hotels and most cars. The constant change between very cold inside and very hot outside affects some new-

*Kuala Lumpur, the capital of Malaysia, is a city steeped in history and tradition yet offers modern amenities and facilities.*

comers' health. Alas, there is nothing more miserable than a snuffling cold in the tropics!

## OFFICE DRESS CODE

Most businesses make their dress code clear to new staff. Suits are common, or else long-sleeved shirts and tie, for men, long-sleeved dress or blouse and skirts for ladies. Many executives keep a coat (and a tie!) somewhere in the office. These can be slipped on if unexpected visitors arrive, senior government officials, Ministers, local notables. Cheerful informality is seen as disrespectful by some older Malaysians — "called on that chap Brown the other day, and he received me just as he was, shirt-sleeves rolled up to his elbows and collar wide open!"

In an air-conditioned office, coats and ties are no hardship. But even the engineer in a site office constructed of mostly reed mats and fresh air is expected to be "properly dressed" if a VIP turns up!

Malaysian government officers wear name tags. The Prime Minister as well as his office boy is tagged for easy identification. Make use of this system: memorize the name of the person at Immigration who's just disappeared with your passport. Half an hour later, when you wonder what's happened to the vital document, you can ask after "Encik Ahmadi" rather than "the man who took my passport out through that door..."

In many business firms, the middle-level staff wear uniforms. Malaysians like uniforms anyway; working outfits help a person save his or her own clothing expenses and are thus quite popular.

## LEARNING THE ROPES

The Malaysian workforce is well educated. Middle and upper-level local executives have studied at business colleges at home and abroad. The general business language is English, though it is an advantage to have a working knowledge of Malay.

Expatriates who come to work in Malaysia have an employment contract and a work permit before entering the country. This means that everything is in order and he starts work on Monday morning... or else he starts hanging around a government office scouting for just one more signature on one more piece of paper.

This doesn't happen often, but it can happen. Newly arrived staff in a big government department may find that the person to whom they were ordered to report has been "transferred outstation" a few weeks ago, or he's at a conference in Canada, or on sick leave, and nobody else is competent (or daring) enough to start John Smith on his new duties.

The best thing for Smith is not to get vociferously annoyed. Things will eventually work out. He does, it is true, waste time; if he can't take that philosophically he's posted to the wrong part of the world. He will spend many more frustrating hours trying to get a seal, a signature, a permit, an essential piece of paper, before his two-year stint is up. The person who's supposed to attend to the business is, according to his secretary, "engaged on the line", "not in", "outstation" or "overseas", and there is nobody else who could possibly touch or even look at the papers.

This is one of the reasons why a newcomer is taken to every reception, every cocktail party, every function of any kind where he can socially meet the people he will be dealing with in business.

Many business houses also assign a "counterpart" to newly arrived officers, an experienced person who will show them the ropes, guide them about protocol and "our house style". This applies to locally recruited staff too. If for some reason a new expatriate has to find his own way around the office jungle, he is well advised to consult older staff members even if in the chain of command they are his inferiors. The Chief Clerk may be a mine of information and office gossip, some of which is essential knowledge for a newcomer.

## A ROSE BY ANY OTHER NAME

Malaysians exchange cards even at social functions. Always carry a few with you, and hand a card politely to a person who is offering you one of his. Offer and accept a visiting card with the right hand loosely supported by the left, or with both hands, and study the one you receive for five seconds. A touchy person will be offended if his card is casually taken and tucked into a pocket.

Visiting cards should provide sufficient information at a glance; the personal name in clear print, the status or job title, the name of your firm or institution. Don't make the managing director of a possible business partner fumble for his glasses because he can't read the tiny print on your card!

Many expats find it difficult to remember Malaysian names. It is a good idea to scrutinize the visiting card carefully on first receiving it. Read the name respectfully and ask: "Is this how you pronounce it?" The owner will repeat it if you had it wrong; maybe a little explanation will follow — it's actually the Mandarin version of my family name, which means this or that — and this will help you to fix the name in memory.

After returning home from a function, many expats (for that matter, many Malaysians) go through all the cards they have received and recall the face that goes with each. This is to make sure they will remember the person next time they meet.

Malaysians are usually rather formal at first meeting. Don't invite a newly-met stranger to "call me Jack" unless the person who is introducing you is a personal mutual friend. To a conservative Malaysian, the casual approach indicates that you may be a good fellow but hardly a serious person.

If a Malaysian man is introduced to you as "Tuan Haji", "Doctor", "Datuk", "Tan Sri" or "Tun", address him by this title, which

is not a substitute for Mister or Encik. A foreign doctor called John Jefferson may take a while to get used to being addressed as "Dr John" rather than Dr Jefferson.

A Malaysian man may or may not introduce his wife if she is not immediately at his elbow, though you are expected to bow in her direction if she is pointed out. If it is necessary that you call her something and the lady has not been introduced by name, you can call her "Mrs Tan", "Mrs Wong", etc, after the husband's name.

The wife of Halim bin Abdullah can be called Mrs Halim at a pinch. This is not strictly speaking correct, but acceptable in an English conversation. She is actually "Mdm Rosinah" or "Puan Rosinah", her own name, but you have no way of knowing that if she hasn't been properly introduced. Just don't call a Malay woman after her husband's second name — Halim Abdullah's wife isn't Mrs Abdullah. Halim is the son of Abdullah, "Mrs Abdullah" is Halim's mother.

The wife of a Datuk is addressed as "Datin", the wife of a Tan Sri as "Puan Sri", the wife of a "Tun" as "Toh Puan." These titles may be used without personal names. Tuan Haji's wife may or may not be a Hajjah; if she wears a white muslin veil or cap she has performed the pilgrimage and is entitled to the honorific "Puan Hajjah". When in doubt err on the side of giving a superfluous title rather than omitting one due.

A well-trained secretary always ushers a person into her employer's office, or puts through phone calls, with a clearly pronounced introduction not omitting titles. Names matter.

Malaysians will go to great lengths to oblige a friend or acquaintance. A faceless Smith, though perfectly entitled to that signature on that document, is left waiting without much compunction. John, Old Chap! on the other hand is invited to walk right in. Please wait for a minute while my secretary gets the file — look, there're two more papers you need for this...no no, my office boy can get them for you! he'll pick them up from Wisma Whatsoever on his motorbike and take them to your office when I've signed all copies. And how're Mary and the kids...?

## HIGH DAYS AND HOLIDAYS

Anyone who does much business outside Kuala Lumpur has got to learn to make allowance for long distances, plane delays, and deep contemplation of the inside walls of airports. When planning the week's itinerary, remember that in Kedah, Kelantan and Trengganu Friday is the weekly holiday, not Sunday; Thursday is the half-day, Saturday and Sunday are ordinary working days.

Aliens travelling between East and West Malaysia need to carry a valid international passport. On this route, an air passenger is penalized if he changes his flight plans within less than 24 hours; "catching the next plane" can be an expensive business if it's not the one he was booked on.

At busy times, near Chinese New Year, Christmas, Hari Raya and the school holidays, East-West flights are booked weeks ahead, months if a trip is really important. This is the season for getting bounced off a plane if the reservation hasn't been confirmed, re-confirmed and re-re-confirmed. In West Malaysia, travellers have the choice between the plane, the bus and the train. Once you're "lost in Borneo", well, there you are! and you won't get back to civilized parts until an airline — any airline — takes pity on you.

## NEGOTIATING A DEAL

Business is business the world over. Malaysian businessmen appear cautious to their Western friends, impetuous to the Japanese — the difference is one of style.

It is not etiquette to go straight to the point when commencing negotiations. Tea or coffee is served, which it is uncouth to refuse even if in the course of a morning's calls the visitor has already had three cups. Small talk starts things off, each party saying nice things about the other's country, national leaders, climate and productions;

211

from there the actual topic of conversation is reached obliquely.

After what he considers a preliminary discussion, a Malaysian often says he would like to "talk the matter over with my partners" whether he has any or not. Expatriates who complain that their local business acquaintances are not straightforward in their dealings fail to understand this. "Yes" in Malaysia means, "Yes, provided that..."; "No" stands for "No, unless...". An Oxford graduate won't say "Wait see first!" the way his unlettered compatriot in the smoked fish business does, but they both share the same feeling. If pressed for an immediate answer it may be negative because a Malaysian businessman doesn't want to commit himself rashly.

The businessman who is introducing a product or project to a prospective buyer should have a good supply of documents, samples, plans. His Malaysian customer would like to keep a copy, possibly two copies so one can be shown to the aforesaid partners. He will be irritated if he is told that this brochure is just to show to custom- ers — once they've inspected it they can place their orders and the sales rep can stash the information material back in his briefcase. This frugal approach won't make many sales in Malaysia.

A deal is not concluded until it is all down in writing, the per- mits and licences approved, the papers signed and sealed — some- times an auspicious day has been chosen for this final operation. Don't fret and fume about the loss of time. Enjoy the presence of a Buddhist priest and the firing of crackers at the opening of your new business venture instead. Visible impatience or skepticism on your part might be considered inauspicious...

## HANDLE WITH CARE!

Buddhist priests and firecrackers aren't the only religious influences on business in Malaysia. A new arrival here is surprised to see some of the female staff draped in top-to-toe clothing which only leaves their faces and hands free. These are Muslim women of strict prin- ciple; their get-up appears strange to the newcomer but wisecracks on the topic are not appreciated. Some men come to work wearing black velvet caps, the *songkok,* especially on Friday.

Muslim workers must be given time off and a place to perform their devotions. The works canteen must be *halal* (serve kosher food) or at least have a *halal* section. Toilets must have facilities for hygienic ablutions. Few newly arrived expatriates have to arrange for any of these things, but they should refrain from commenting on them critically. "Water taps inside the toilet cubicles? What the hell for...?" The people who use the toilets know what the taps are for; John Smith can simply ignore them and use paper for the same purpose.

Some Malaysian women, Muslim and otherwise, act extremely shy or at least preserve the very strictest decorum in the presence of men; this applies particularly to the lower ranks of employees. An expatriate alone in a lift may be surprised, or hurt, if a woman waiting on another floor glances through the door and refuses to join him in the same lift.

Yes, this is discrimination — not because he is a foreigner, but because he is a man! The poor girl's reputation could be compromised (and her workmates wouldn't let her forget it for six months) if she entered a closed cubicle alone with a man for the 10 seconds the average lift journey takes.

Seasoned expats sometimes advise newly arrived bachelor officers to preserve extra-cool demeanour with all the girls in the office. Friendly remarks not pertaining to business, jokes, innocent invitations to a meal ("it was the least I could do after I'd asked her to type those reports until nearly 9 p.m.!") may be misunderstood. How can a fellow tell when he's gone too far? When a respectable papa in his best suit is ushered into the office for an urgent private interview...

The truly shy, conservative maiden is not likely to work in a big international company as executive secretary, however. I have not heard of any "close proximity" cases brought against a foreigner dictating business letters to his secretary.

The entertainment media frequently feature stories of the nurse who married the top surgeon, the secretary who married the manager; it is also a stock theme of trash novels which sell very well in Malaysia. The vulgar version celebrates the nurse who has an affair with the married top surgeon, the secretary who has an affair with the married manager. In real Malaysian life, such romances occur about as frequently as elsewhere.

There is a type of girl, now less numerous than she used to be, who is determined to catch an expat. Any expat...and he will carry her off into the rosy sunset of TV soap affluence. An extant middle-aged wife is not necessarily seen as an obstacle by this prettily plumed bird of prey! The girl may be found working in offices, hanging around places of entertainment, clubs or bars where Europeans congregate. She is very free-and-easy at first approach. Once she considers her man secure, she dissolves into tearful trepidation — "my papa would kill me if he knew..!" and makes stormy demands for immediate marriage.

## *HUMOUR IN THE OFFICE*

One definition of fluency in a foreign language is: "If you can tell a joke in the new language and it's funny." The obverse of this wise saw would be, if you can say something serious and it's not funny!

It is not assumed that a foreigner will march into a Malaysian office and start cracking jokes in Malay. But until he has ascertained the exact level of his coworkers' English, he may puzzle or insult them each time he jokes in that language.

Malaysians working in a big business office understand English, more or less well, some of them very well. But they may have radically different ideas of what is funny. In general, Malaysians are a formal people, especially with strangers and newcomers. Unbusinesslike remarks made by a new coworker won't be considered at all humorous, but strange.

Watching new and old Malaysian films, reading the local press and studying cartoons give an indication of what is considered funny here. Horseplay is appreciated among friends, outrageous or ribald slapstick brings the house down in cinemas. Broad humour is strongly visual; verbal humour needs to be polished and witty to be appreciated.

There is much fun and laughter in Malaysia. The newcomer needs to watch and listen for a while before he can actively join in.

## BUSINESS GOLF AND CROCODILES

Business Golf is not a Malaysian invention, but it is as popular here as elsewhere on earth. The clubs are places for people to meet informally. One type of "celebrity hound" spends his or her time on the golf course in hopes of getting practically within swinging reach of the Minister of this or the Sultan of that, "and as I walked out of the showers who should stroll by but Puan Sri..."

Serious business and political deals may well be started at golf clubs, but the final negotiations are conducted in offices.

Businessmen, local and foreign, admit that there is "a certain amount" of corruption in Malaysia. Most have a juicy story to illustrate their point, "but MY company has never paid a bribe, you understand!" If it's any consolation, most consider Malaysia as one of the "cleaner" countries in Southeast Asia.

The whole question of bribes, commissions, spin-offs and perks is shrouded in thick clouds of vagueness. Business companies as well as individual executives are frequently solicited for charitable contributions, for sponsorship of sports or cultural events, for anything and everything. What happens if you say NO?

Is it coincidence that a big contract went to the company that had just made a thumping donation to the local politician's favourite charity? How did the head of a government department that bought 36 four-wheel drive vehicles acquire a deluxe model himself a week after tenders closed? And why is the whole redecoration project of a 12-storey office block handled by a company belonging to the Director's wife?

Expatriates are used to different ideas of what is ethical, and what is not. An Australian is frankly shocked to find that all the plum jobs in his employer's company are held by relatives. "Back home that's called nepotism!" he fumes — and so it is. In Malaysia it's called Taking Care of the Family. An Australian wouldn't dare give jobs to all his cousins because people would talk. A Malaysian wouldn't dare leave his relatives unprovided-for if he can possibly help it, because people would talk.

An expatriate businessman who feels that he has discovered serious, unadorned corruption in high places is free to report the matter to the Anti-Corruption Agency. He is strongly advised against such drastic action unless he has definite evidence, and has discussed the matter with a trusted, knowledgeable local friend.

"In the first three months here, keep your eyes and ears open and your mouth shut!" is the laconic advice given by an Australian businessman in East Malaysia.

The newcomer in the Malaysian business world is often preyed upon by "consultants" who claim they can introduce him to appropriate contacts, assist him in getting a permit where strictly speaking none is obtainable, speed up a slow lot of negotiations — at a price. Variously called "rentier businessmen" or "influence peddlers", these gentry have charming manners, an excellent understanding of western business attitudes, big cars, unlimited hospitality and impeccable sartorial effects. At best, they cost their victim a lot of money; at worst, they may have pulled him and his name into illegal deals!

There are genuine business consultant firms in Malaysia. A newly arrived businessman should check out the credentials of anyone who calls himself "consultant" but prefers conducting business at the local club. For that matter, even posh office premises are no guarantee of respectability! The "consultant" who promises to achieve miracles, the compulsive name-dropper, the persistent caller must be treated with caution. If the deal in question is big, an expatriate does well to check with his Embassy whether they have any knowledge of the consultant, to ask the opinion of local staff and business friends in the same line.

## THE GHOSTBUSTERS

It is possible that the entire female workforce of a factory (or, less commonly, an office) bursts into hysteria after one of their number has "seen something". Such outbreaks sometimes occur in boarding schools or university hostels, too. The something may be a Peeping Tom around the quarters, but most of the girls will take it to be a ghost and act accordingly.

An expatriate is strongly advised to leave the handling of the whole affair to competent local personnel. No way can a hysterical person "snap out of it", it's useless to tell her so. Visible disbelief on her audience's part may only spur her to further efforts.

Measures must be taken to prevent the girls from hurting themselves and each other; emergency ward staff at the local hospital may be called in. A brief ride in an ambulance often does wonders.

In most cases of mass hysteria, the affected premises are closed down for the day and all workers or students are told to go home. Then, competent religious or magic assistance is sought by the local staff in charge. If an expatriate officer is asked to attend the exorcism in person he should do so "to show respect", keeping well in the background and firmly suppressing his feelings about mumbo-jumbo.

The fifteenth day of the seventh lunar month (August-September) is the Hungry Ghosts' Festival, when Chinese Buddhists offer food and entertainment to those who died unknown and unmourned and whose shades are let out of the underworld for the occasion. Office or factory workers may ask for a half-day off, consult local senior staff about the company's policy on such matters. The half-holiday is usually granted; an expat officer may find it interesting to go along and watch the proceedings. Many an elegant highrise building right in the business district of major Malaysian towns has a little red shrine for the convenience of Hungry and general-purpose Ghosts, right there on the premises!

Roughly built red shrines are common at worksites also. Sometimes they are found at the foot of particularly venerable trees. Workers engaged in jungle-clearing may object to felling a banyan tree because it is the abode of ghosts, especially if some of them are orang asli. The aboriginal inhabitants of the Malay Peninsula have strong traditional feelings concerning the sylvan spirits.

Does this mean that the 1000 hectares needed for a new project may be dotted here and there with trees that couldn't be felled? Not really. But it means some caution and diplomacy is needed to preserve the workforce's morale while making sure they do fell those trees in the end. They most likely expect offerings to be placed near the trunks. The foreman or local site engineer is the best man to decide whether a small ceremony is in order, and who should be called in to perform it.

On site as in the office, the expatriate does best to keep his own views on spooks firmly to himself. Scoffing remarks about "shirking work on the pretext of a bloody ghost" won't go down well.

If an expatriate insists that work be carried on as usual without ghost-time taken off he may be able to carry his point. But from then on any accident on the site will be blamed on the person who insulted the supernatural, namely the expatriate who took a firm line.

## THE LAST THINGS

An employee who has lost a family member should be given time off to attend the funeral. If he is in the lower-paid group, a small tip (M$20 – 30) "to help with expenses" is appreciated. The bereaved will inform his boss that his mother has "passed away", not that she has died — direct expressions of death are studiously avoided by Malaysians.

If a colleague or close kin of senior staff has passed away, it is customary to insert a Condolence notice in the local press. Let one of the local staff handle this, and just pay up your share. The wording of such notices is crucial. This applies to letters of condolence if any have to be sent. They should be composed by a staff member of the same race and religion as the deceased: Muslims are piously surmised to Dwell Among Heavenly Beings, Christians are charitably hoped to Rest in Peace, Buddhists have Returned to their Venerable Ancestors.

There should be staff consultation to decide who will attend the funeral or visit a house of mourning. Sombre clothes without jewellery are worn for such occasions.

If the deceased was Muslim, people should visit the house while the body is still there. An expatriate should be accompanied by a Muslim staff member who can quietly guide him as to protocol. On no account kiss the widow! A Christian family would expect an expatriate friend of the deceased to attend the funeral service in Church, possibly follow the procession to the graveyard. Hindu families receive condolatory visits in the house of mourning, as do Buddhists.

Attendance in the cortege is much appreciated by the Chinese family. Neighbours are impressed by a really endless funeral procession which snarls up traffic for hours. It shows the deceased was universally liked and respected, and it gives "face" to his descendants.

Should a leading politician or ruler pass away, the heads of government departments and leading business firms are expected to attend the obsequies. They will be fully briefed by protocol officers on what to wear, where to walk, what to do.

# CULTURAL QUIZ

## SITUATION 1

You are in a small coffee shop, trying to order bottled lemonade. The waiter looks extremely dull, mumbles "yes" and "no" without much regard to what you're saying, and doesn't seem to make any effort to understand you.

    a) You grab his arm and give it a gentle shake.
    b) You raise your voice.
    c) You go over to the refrigerator and choose your own.
    d) You stomp out of the shop, complaining loudly.

### Comments

    a) Not only useless in the present situation, but seen as "pawing" particularly if the two parties are of opposite sexes.

    b) Not much use. If he doesn't understand, he doesn't understand. It is a good idea to learn the brand names of your preferred flavours; lemonade is marketed as "Sprite" or "Seven-Up", for instance.

c) This is the best solution, but do it gracefully. Your demeanour can say "Sorry, we don't seem to understand each other!" or "With an idiot like you this is the only way!" quite clearly; the man may not understand English but he understands face and body language.

Point to the various bottles (with your whole hand, not one finger) and ask: Is this orange flavour? Lemon? etc

d) If you're not planning to come this way again, all right. In towns where there are lots of small coffee shops, you'll find a drink elsewhere.

## SITUATION 2

Your child attends a local music school. One day he comes home with a theory exercise book in which his correct answers are marked wrong.

a) You ask the child if he wants you to talk to his teacher.

b) You ring the school director and complain.

c) You go to the school and confront the teacher.

## Comments

a) Do this before you take any action at all. Maybe the questions were ambiguous, the student's handwriting illegible. Your child, maybe the only foreign student in his group, already "stands out". A ruckus raised on his behalf will mark him further, and may make him unpopular with his fellow-students.

b) Not without consulting the child first! In Malaysian society, respect and deference for teachers is fairly strongly ingrained. We don't imagine they are infallible, but we try not to criticize them. The director will tick off the teacher in question, she in turn may "take it out" on the child whose parent complained, making her lose face.

221

c) Do this nicely, and privately so no other teachers or students know about it.

Do not burst into the studio during a group lesson and expose the teacher's abysmal ignorance; your child will not enjoy his music lessons after such a performance.

If she's really incompetent, consider finding another school or teacher.

## SITUATION 3

You get into a taxi outside one of KL's big hotels and give your destination, about five minutes' drive away. The driver asks: "Ten dollars all right?"

a) You get out, slam the door and look for another taxi.

b) You say: "Yes, all right", take the trip and pay up.

c) You say: "Would you use the meter, please!" in firm tones.

d) You get out, take the cab's number and report the driver to the Malaysian Tourism Promotion Board.

## Comments

a) This is assuming that you know what the fare should be. The driver will (we hope) get the message that not all expatriates are willing to be taken for a ride.

b) As taxi meters are mandatory, you should never do this. Use option (c).

c) Correct. All KL taxis are fitted with meters which have to be used. Some drivers try to cash in on a foreigner's ignorance.

d) Start by threatening to do all this. The driver will probably mumble and grumble a bit and then turn the meter on; it shows $1.50 when first engaged.

The MTPB's phone number is on every tourist pamphlet. The few rude taxi drivers in KL would turn into perfect gentlemen at once if they knew their misdemeanours were sure to be reported.

## SITUATION 4

A few friends are coming for afternoon tea. Your children are playing with their puppy in the room where the tea will be served. The frisky little animal is perfectly harmless and never bites, though it loves licking such hands and feet as it can reach, or carrying people's shoes around the garden. Before your guests arrrive,

   a) You tell your children to be nice with their little guests and let them play with the puppy.

   b) You tell your arriving guests that the puppy doesn't bite, they need not be afraid of it.

   c) You tie the puppy up where the children can see it and play with it if they like.

   d) You lock or tie the puppy up, out of sight.

### Comments

   a) No, keep it out of sight. Explain to your children why their pet cannot appear in public when you have guests.

b) No, keep it out of sight. Some of your friends may be Muslim; they are not frightened that the dog will bite them, but their religion does not permit them to touch or be touched by one.

c) If the guests' children are not supposed to touch dogs, this is placing temptation rather cruelly in their way. The puppy is also more likely to whine or bark if he can see his usual playmates, but is tied up.

d) Correct. Admittedly there are some Muslims who keep dogs, but that is their own decision. You can't foist your tastes on those who don't.

## *SITUATION 5*

The driver behind you couldn't stop fast enough and crashes into you. Both cars are badly dented. The other driver's passenger walks to nearby shops to call the police.

A tow truck pulls up. Its crew assure you that your car won't be able to move. Lucky they are here! Their garage does panelbeating and engine repairs; a few persons in the accumulating crowd assure you that it's one of the best outfits in town. You are offered a form to sign "and we'll tow the car to the workshop as soon as the police have finished".

a) You sign, relieved to have help at hand so readily.

b) You decline to sign anything but go off to ring your own garage.

c) You ask the police officer's advice.

d) You sign because the driver of the other damaged car is also signing; being local, maybe he knows the workshop.

## *Comments*

a) You are almost certainly being taken for a ride, and an expensive ride at that. NEVER sign anything unless you've read through and fully understand it.

b) is the right answer. After the police report has been made, test whether your car is really unable to move. If you need a tow, ring your own garage or a local friend; don't forget to inform your insurance company.

c) He may be too busy to pay very much attention, but it's worth a try. If the tow truck operator is a known sharp practitioner, the police are likely to know him.

d) The poor chap is as upset and dazed as you are. Exchange information about your respective insurance companies but don't sign anything.

## *SITUATION 6*

You are entertaining a valued client in your office. Certain papers are needed. You ring your office boy to bring them. He brings a wrong file; you reject it and ask him to look for the right one. He brings another wrong file, and then a third.

a) You stomp out of the room to get the correct file, which you show to your office boy as you bring it. You tell him what you think of lazy careless, etc, Malaysians, "no wonder your country is still so backward, and I told you the file was on the second shelf", etc, etc.

b) You call your secretary on the intercom and ask her to locate the file, then send the office boy to go and get it.

c) You excuse yourself and leave the room to get the file; after the guest has left you say a few words to the office boy.

d) You ask your secretary to locate the file and bring it in.

## *Comments*

a) This will upset the boy terribly, especially if your voice can be heard in other parts of the office. Ticking him off in front of others makes him "lose face", you shouldn't do it!

b) This is the face-saving solution; the boy doesn't have to stand there while somebody else performs the task he should have. There's nothing to stop you from giving him a quiet talking-to afterwards. If he habitually does wrong things, there's nothing wrong with replacing him, either.

c) Next-best to b)

d) Better than a) but not as good as b), it exposes the office boy to the "shame" of somebody else publicly performing a task he was "too stupid" to do.

227

## SITUATION 7

Your husband is a technical officer with a big government department. A woman whose husband is a contractor sometimes working for your husband's department is very nice to you.

She takes you out for meals, invites you to visit her house. On your birthday she gives you a valuable diamond brooch.

a) You hand the brooch back to Milly, indignantly accusing her of trying to bribe your husband in this way.

b) You take it as a token of friendship and proudly show it to your other friends.

c) You keep quiet about it for a while.

d) You thank her profusely, but assure her that you couldn't possibly keep it; invent a superstitious dread of diamonds if necessary.

## Comments

a) It is very difficult to say which presents are meant as bribes, and which aren't. Even if the accusation is true, you shouldn't make it to her face.

b) If your last gift to her was worth about the same, you are justified in keeping hers. But be prepared for questions from the Anti-Corruption Agency at a later date.

c) Inform your husband before accepting a valuable present. Somebody may be trying to "frame" him. If Milly's husband has tendered for a multimillion contract two weeks ago, he will probably insist that the gift be returned.

d) This is the graceful way out. It doesn't hurt feelings, but it gives Milly the message that you would accept flowers, fruits or trifles but not valuables.

The same caution is necessary with very expensive gifts offered to your children.

## SITUATION 8

Your husband has invited a few business friends for an informal dinner at home. He is very vague about what they will or won't eat, saying in true husband-fashion: "...oh, anything..."

a) You prepare a formal sit-down dinner of five courses with all the right wines.

b) You prepare a buffet because it's easier to serve; as you are rather adept at making pork-pies you put these at one end of the table; the Muslims will of course eat from the other end.

c) You prepare a buffet with neither pork nor beef because you never know who eats what.

d) You ring your husband's secretary and ask her to call all the guests and find out what, if any, food taboos they observe.

## *Comments*

a) No, not unless you have met and shared meals with everyone of the expected guests.

b) Tactless to the point of useless; raised pork pies are a specialty dish that many people won't recognize at a glance. The hostess would have to stand beside the table warning each guest off!

c) The simplest solution; besides chicken and fish there are some delicious vegetarian dishes, and if there's enough variety you can risk something cheesy.

d) The best solution if you are in contact with the secretary, and she is in contact with the persons invited.

# CULTURE TIPS A – Z

**Ang mo.** Literally red-hairs, it refers to persons of Caucasian descent. Other terms are *Mat Salleh* and *Orang Puteh.* The latter, sometimes abberivated to O.P.,"white person", is used in polite conversation. The other terms are considered somewhat vulgar.

**Barber shop.** May be a place to get an innocent haircut and shampoo (for which see **S**), or it may be a front for a brothel. Even in respectable establishments the barbers are often girls, so look out for Warning Signs:

\* The shop's opening hours are from afternoon till late at night;

\* Customers are led to private screened cubicles to be attended to;

\* There is a disproportionate number of girls compared to the number of barber chairs.

**Crackers.** Be warned: if you are in Malaysia during the Chinese New Year season, there will be almost constant cracker-fire, rockets and other explosives, working up to a crescendo near midnight of the First Day and on the Fifteenth. Despite warnings and official prohibitions on certain types of crackers, children handle these dangerous toys with predictable results and sometimes loss of life. Boys amuse themselves by tossing fireworks into houses or passing cars. If you live in or drive through a neighbourhood with pyromaniacal tendency, keep your windows closed!

**Hair and head.** Neither may be touched by a stranger. Don't pat children on the head. If you can't keep your hands off a chubby cherub, chuck him under the chin or pat his cheek — he'll probably burst into loud bellows on impact while his granny reassuringly tells him not to be afraid of the *ang mo kow*.

**Karaoke, or "empty orchestra".** A Japanese invention that is taking Malaysia by storm. The taped accompaniment to current pop songs blares from a loudspeaker, patrons take the mike and sing their hearts out to entertain the crowd. As everyone present hopes to get a turn at the mike eventually, nobody can afford to be too critical of the other singers' performance. A new complex in KL is entirely devoted to this form of massacring music. Karaoke is an entertainment warmly recommended for bathtub Carusos and the tone-deaf.

**Makan.** The Malay word everyone picks up means Eat! Even resident expatriates invite each other: "Let's go for makan!" snacks or a meal, usually at the food stalls; "makan time" denotes dinner time.

**Nightclubs.** Those good folks who consider KL "dull" obviously don't know where to look, as there is plenty of nightlife around. It is advisable to go in a group including locals who know the place until you have found your way around a little. As elsewhere on earth, some nightclubs are very expensive, others are "dives", still others have their regular fight at 1.30 a.m. We cater for all tastes!

**Prostitution.** It exists in Malaysia, though it is banned by the Malaysian government. This means, in plain terms, that there is no health control of the persons engaged in the trade. All types of VD do exist in this country, and there have been a number of AIDS cases in recent years — buyer beware!

**Queers**. The word "gay" is gaining acceptance. There is no open "gay culture" here, in fact many homosexuals are encouraged to marry by their families because "people might talk."

**Pondan**. The local term used to describe transvestites. In certain areas of the bigger towns they can be obtrusive. Some are so well dressed and made-up that it is difficult to detect their real gender!

Large numbers of Malaysians will flatly refuse to believe that there is such a thing as a gay female; maybe it is wiser to leave those in ignorance who consider it bliss.

**Rain.** Yes we've got lots of it but no it never lasts long. A collapsible umbrella is a useful thing to carry in a shopping bag or briefcase, or keep in the back of the car, just in case...

**Raincoats or ponchos.** They are uncomfortable because of the climate. Even a short walk in such an air-tight cover will make its wearer very hot.

**Shampoo.** May surprise you the first time you have it in a Malaysian "Beauty Saloon". While the customer sits in the chair, a girl squirts small amounts of water on her head, then applies shampoo and starts to work up a lather. More water, more shampoo are added until the whole head is covered in suds. Some girls rub so energetically that a woman not used to this type of massage fears her scalp may come off; many local customers prefer it this way. If she's too vigorous for your liking, tell her to stop.

Only after thorough lathering is the customer led to a basin where her hair will be rinsed.

**Telephone.** Public phones are found all over the place. An orange public phone is operated by coins, a yellow one needs a Phone Card (available in nearby shops) to make it work. Counter-top pay phones are found in some shops; the older model of these can only be used for local calls.

**Uniforms**. We love them! Not only the Cabinet and Civil Service have dress uniforms (mercifully not worn in the office), even the Cabinet Wives may be seen disporting themselves in uniform outfits. The girls helping out at a *kampung* wedding start by getting blouses of the same colour, members of political parties wear their allegiance on their sleeves in an overall print pattern. Schoolchildren, bus conductors, checkout girls, municipal dog catchers, waitresses, anybody who is somebody wears uniform. A word of warning: the more creative thieves invest in natty overalls to gain easy entry into houses. Bona-fide water and power company employees have a security tag as well as a uniform. When in doubt, ring the utility company to check that their workers are really supposed to be doing something inside your house.

**Water.** Should be abundant in a high-rainfall area. Sometimes it's not; there are seasons and regions with water rationing, shut-offs for certain periods, or the unexplained trickling dry of taps. Look for ample roof cistern storage space when renting a house. Have a few clean buckets handy, one in each bathroom and in the kitchen, which can be filled if there's a drought scare.

Remember that sensible water management in every private household helps to conserve the available total.

**X-rated material.** Banned in Malaysia even if it is available under the counter. Every now and then a shop selling or lending it is raided with loud trumpetings of moral outrage; private homes are usually safe but there may be a "tip-off" from someone who wasn't invited to the very private video show in a friend's house. Foreign residents play it safe by not importing anything that could be objectionable. The final say on what is obscene and what is not lies with the magistrate or judge, normally a very conservative person.

**Zeal.** A good thing in a good cause and a very bad one if misapplied. Malaysians don't want to hear a wild-eyed foreigner tell them how they should administer their country, conduct their elections, perform their devotions and protect their environment, for instance!

# BIBLIOGRAPHY

*Malaysia Year Book,* Ministry of Information, Malaysia, Kuala Lumpur (published annually).

*The Making of Modern Malaysia and Singapore,* N. J. Ryan, Oxford University Press, Kuala Lumpur 1969. A comprehensive history of Malaysia from the Early Stone Age to the mid-60s, written in clear elegant English.

*The Golden Khersonese,* Isabella Bird, John Murray, London 1883, Oxford reprint 1986. This is a travelogue written by a daring Victorian woman with a keen eye and a sharp tongue; a very interesting piece of I-was-there history.

*The Malay Archipelago,* A.R. Wallace (1869), Graham Brash reprint, Singapore 1983. An informative book on travel and natural history by the co-discoverer of the Theory of Evolution.

*Cultures of the World — Malaysia,* Heidi Munan, Times Editions, Singapore 1990. An illustrated general reference work on Malaysia, written for young teens.

*Kuala Lumpur 1880 –1895,* J.M.Gullick (1955), Pelanduk Publications, Kuala Lumpur 1988. A detailed and fascinating history of Malaysia's capital in its early years, with period illustrations and maps.

*The Soul of Malaya,* H. Fauconnier, English Translation 1931, Oxford University Press reprint 1985. This is a "mood book" of Malaya before the war, sensitively written from a strongly western point of view.

*Ah King and Other Stories,* S. Maugham, Oxford University Press, Singapore 1986.

*The Sime Darby Food Lovers' Guide,* Sime Darby, Kuala Lumpur 1990. Don't leave home without it!

*The Pirate Wind,* O. Rutter, Oxford University Press 1986 (reprint). The name says it all; this historical study evaluates the influence of Borneo and Sulu pirates on Insulindian trade in the last 200 years.

*The People of the Weeping Forest,* J. Ave and V. King, Rijksmuseum voor Volkerkunde, Leiden 1986. A new and sensitive appraisal of the island Borneo as a whole.

*The Sarawak Chinese,* J.M. Chin, Oxford University Press, Kuala Lumpur 1981. Sarawak history from the Chinese point of view, with an interesting chapter on pre-Brooke history.

*Sabah — The First Hundred Years,* C. Leong, Percetakan Man Yang Muda, Kuala Lumpur 1982. This history of Sabah, written in a fluent style, covers the essential and omits the tedious.

*The Birds of Borneo,* B. Smythies, Sabah Society, Kuala Lumpur 1984. A classic Borneo wildlife study reduced to convenient carrying size.

# THE AUTHOR

Heidi Munan was born Adelheid Oettli in Switzerland. Her family migrated to New Zealand, where she attended University and Teachers' College.

Fate in the person of Sidi Munan took her to Sarawak in 1965. The couple have two children.

Heidi Munan taught for a number of years but eventually retired to become a part-time journalist and full-time mother, daughter-in-law, aunt, niece, granny, cook, driver, nurse and general trouble-shooter to an over-extended family.

In her rare free moments, Heidi is a private researcher at the Sarawak Museum, and contributor to a number of local and overseas publications. She takes a keen interest in the varied cultures of her home State, particularly in the language and literature of the Iban people.

In collaboration with Malaysian composer Julia Chong, Heidi has produced Sarawak's first operetta, *Life in the Jungle,* and a number of shorter occasional pieces. She is also the author of *Culture Shock Borneo, Cultures of the World – Malaysia* (both published by Times Books International), *Sarawak Crafts* (OUP) and short collections of Borneo folk tales.

# INDEX